Praise for

CLEAR AS CLAY

"Whether lampooning a mother's clumsy love, reliving dreaded wedding planning, crafting a scatological paean to empathy, or lauding the benefits of a safety coffin, Patrick Lombardi's essays reveal the transformative potential of the trivial, the wonder that is a meatloaf dinner or an oil change. Deftly interweaving humor and grace, the absurd and the sober, his free-ranging recollections read like Norman Rockwell moments sketched by R. Crumb."

— David R. Roth,
award-winning author of
The Femme Fatale Hypothesis

"Patrick Lombardi skillfully mines the mundane for fodder for well-crafted essays on adulthood. Lombardi has turned seemingly innocuous moments—from waiting in line at an ice cream shop to calling a plumber as a new homeowner—into a side-splittingly funny book. You'll root for Lombardi as he fumbles through this phase of his life, and you might see yourself in it—especially if you also happen to be from New Jersey."

— Kerri Sullivan,
New Jersey Fan Club
and founder of Jersey Collective

"Patrick Lombardi's essays are full of insight, heart, and humor. You will be touched and moved, and you will laugh out loud. Highly recommended!"

— Dr. Lise Deguire, Psy.D.,
award-winning author of *Flashback Girl:
Lessons on Resilience from a Burn Survivor*

"Patrick Lombardi brings a storyteller's eye to the everyday, elevating ordinary experiences into tales we can all relate to with wit, grace, and humor."

— Nancy Norbeck,
Follow Your Curiosity podcast

"Patrick Lombardi has found a way to turn humor into a tool. Like a hot knife flawlessly cutting through butter, his sardonic wit uses the force of osmosis to quickly permeate skin, tissue, and nerve to hit the funny bone—and hard! Get ready to lose yourself in story and find yourself again feeling a little lighter, and who doesn't need that? The reason to get *Clear as Clay* is clear as glass."

— Marc Kaye,
comedian, musician, and author

This is a

READER'S BOOK CLUB EDITION

of

CLEAR AS CLAY

provoking life's moldable moments

by

PATRICK LOMBARDI

At the end of this book, find:
A conversation with the author
Book recommendations
Discussion questions to enhance your book club

This guy also wrote

Junk Sale

The New Jersey Food Truck Cookbook

CLEAR AS CLAY

provoking life's

moldable moments

PATRICK LOMBARDI

New Jersey

A version of "The Problem Is . . ." was performed for the 2023 Bucks
County Storytelling Series.

Edited by Matthew Schuman

Library of Congress Control Number: 2024912128

ISBN: 979-8-9898193-0-0

Cover image: Keen Observer Clayhead by Aman Khanna, claymen.in
Cover fonts: Nexa Rust Sans Black by Svetoslav Simov / Fontfabric,
fontfabric.com; Otto by Kevin Richey

Printed and bound in the United States of America

For my incredible wife, Christine,
who has heard me start a sentence with
"So I have this idea . . ." about 742 times
and still hasn't served me divorce papers

CONTENTS

CLEAR

AS

CLAY

SAMPLING SAFARI

A spoonful of dessert, no matter how small, is equivalent to a Jeep tour through the Tijuca rainforest. It's saturated with so many levels of absorbing disparateness that one has to take a moment to appreciate the experience before it disappears. Then, and only then, can one move onto the next tour—or *spoonful*.

Each dessert is a different journey. Lava cake is your Mayon Volcano outing. Doughnuts are whitewater rafting through the boulder-strewn span of the Tuolumne River. Fruit cake is a North Korean detention center. (Not every dessert is a holiday.)

Ice cream, though, is a sightseeing tour through the tropical islands of Hawaii. It's the crystalline beaches caressing your body; it's 'Opaeka'a Falls hugged by lush forest; it's a psychedelic submarine ride alongside kaleidoscope fish. It's a soulful paradise, especially when it's gelato—my favorite.

I used to make special trips to a place about a half an hour from my house specifically for its dark chocolate gelato. The shop offered a dozen different flavors in addition to frozen yogurt, but I stuck with just the one. I ordered the largest size, which was only sixteen ounces and far too small. If it were served in an industrial vat made for mixing cement, maybe then I would've been satisfied. But for the time, I settled for the one flavor, which could barely fill a sippy cup. Even when I'd go multiple times a week, I never got sick of it.

The gelateria was set back in a smaller version of your average mall. There was just enough space for it inside a narrow alcove between a burger joint and the public restrooms. The first time I passed the place, I walked right by it, unaware that it even existed. It wasn't until I was traveling back, in the opposite direction, that it caught my eye.

It was just an ice cream counter. You could've stepped inside the open entryway by the cash register, but only a few feet. This area, which had the confinement of an airplane bathroom, allowed you enough space to survey the toppings behind a thin shield of sneeze glass. It only offered a variety of diced nuts, and there was barely any room for *that*. If you brought a squirrel in with you, he'd be thrilled. The glass case that contained the gelato was a bit more conspicuous. It jutted out into the mall's hallway, blocking traffic like those souvenir stands on any Jersey Shore boardwalk.

When I was bored, I used to look up pictures of gelato online, wondering what special flavors were being offered that day. The surreptitious site visits were meant to be brief and informative, but I could spend long, pleasurable hours appreciating the art that is sweet frozen-dairy dessert. If it was accompanied by brioche or sitting atop a fresh waffle cone, my heart could really get racing.

To say I have a sweet tooth is like saying an orca has a taste for fish, or that a hoarder is into collectables. Sure, you'd be on the right track, but you'd be nowhere near the finish line.

I regularly came to the mall for this sole reason. There was a Barnes & Noble anchored at one end, and I enjoyed perusing several sections before making my way deeper into the mall for some gelato. But nothing except dessert seemed to matter. Still, I migrated at a turtle's pace. The slower I moved, the more I built the anticipation. The greater the anticipation, the more satisfying the gelato. Maybe that wasn't entirely true, but I needed to tell myself that, especially when I was stuck at the end of a long line.

A woman cut in front of me once when I was treading the hallway toward this dairy heaven. I hadn't stepped in line—a line which did not yet exist—so truthfully she had done nothing wrong. She dragged her feet as she sauntered toward the counter. I could hear the soles of her shoes grate the vinyl tiled floor like long puffs of flatulence behind the filter of an adult diaper. I followed pathetically behind. When the only employee at the counter greeted her, she said nothing in reply. She simply contemplated the variety of flavors in their effusive displays, and I expected her to press her face against the glass, eyes wide and tongue out.

After a few seconds of silence, the man behind the counter, whose nametag read CRAIG, said, "You can try some flavors, if you'd like."

I feared that a man in this position made this mistake daily. In my opinion, that statement should never be uttered. If a customer isn't aware that she can try any flavor she'd like at an ice cream parlor, then she should be doomed to pick her flavors blindly and suffer the consequences. Charles Darwin said something like that, I think.

I saw her arms hop into the air in excitement. In a heavy accent that I couldn't quite peg—which very well could've been New Jerseyan—she said, "I wan to try da vanilla."

Craig grabbed a tiny pink spoon from a container and carved out a heaping dose of white gelato. With a smile, he handed it to her, and she took it from him and devoured the sample with the force of an anteater snorting insects. I saw her nod, and in response, Craig nodded, too. "So a small vanilla then?" he suggested.

She shook her head. "I wan to try da coffee one," she told Craig, and he used a new spoon to scoop out some beige gelato. It was the same hue as my grandfather's old Members Only jacket that he wore when he went outside to have a smoke during the fall. Instead of discarding her dirty spoon into the bucket in front of her, the woman moved it to her left hand and used her right hand to take the new one from Craig. She smacked her lips after tasting the sample. "Dis one too sweet." After a brief pause, she said, "I wan to try da watermelon."

I flailed my arms outward and let them slap against my thighs when they fell. *Is she kidding me?*

"Well, the watermelon's actually sweeter than the coffee flavor," Craig warned.

"Das okay," she replied. She moved the second dirty spoon to her left hand and took the new one with her right. She tasted the spoonful of watermelon gelato and began to shake her head. Her frizzy brown hair whipped back and forth. "No, no, no. Let me try da cookie cream."

I huffed once, loud enough for her to hear my impatience expel through my nostrils. That apparently wasn't enough to get her moving.

Craig continued to scoop flavor after flavor for the woman until she was holding a collection of around eight used spoons in her left hand. He repeatedly tipped the open end of the mini receptacle in her direction, saying, "You can throw your spoons in this bucket, ma'am."

"I wan to try da sea salt caramel," she'd say in response, as she moved another spoon to her left hand. I assumed she was keeping them as souvenirs. Perhaps she didn't have such tiny spoons in her kitchen and wanted to bring them home, one for each member of her extended family, every neighbor she's ever met, and her mailman and paperboy. Or maybe she was just in desperate need of small plastic spoons, and this was the perfect opportunity to stock up. She had licked each one clean, and I felt sorry for anyone who happened to have tea at her house, because I suspected that this was as much washing as those spoons would get before being put back to use. I couldn't imagine that this person—someone who held up an entire line of people by sampling every flavor of gelato—would care more about the cleanliness of utensils than the sanctity of our time. Even though those two characteristics have no connection whatsoever, the sentiment just didn't jive with me, and I strongly disliked her for no rational reason.

A line had started forming behind us when she was on just her second sample, but this woman obviously didn't seem to mind. She likely didn't even notice, as she was too enthralled by the free samples—or the tiny spoons—to turn around and see the delays she was causing. I was upset that she didn't even feign interest. She'd just devour a tiny spoonful and ask for another flavor. She savored nothing, and it disgusted me. Samples are not meant to be consumed and immediately forgotten. But this woman appeared to have no idea.

There was a couple holding hands with a young boy and girl directly behind me in line. The children looked to be around five years old. After a few minutes of waiting, the boy began to stir. Every few seconds, I heard tiny feet stomp behind me. When the woman in front of me asked for her tenth sample, I turned around to see that the boy's face had started to suffuse with a warm shade of pink. If he wasn't going to start screaming, I was. When it came to dessert, I was no better than a kindergartener, and this lady was about to find that out.

After her tenth sample, the woman once again shook her head. "You know, I go wid frozen yogurt."

I just then noticed my hand had been curled into a fist, and I relaxed it. Punching this woman actually never crossed my mind. I'm not a violent person, but I also would never risk getting thrown out of the mall and losing my place in line at a gelateria, especially after watching someone try ten samples of a product she had no intention of purchasing.

Craig let out a sigh of relief and moved over toward the frozen yogurt cups. "What flavor?" he asked, making sure to omit his line about trying free samples. The woman told him which flavor she was craving, which crushed-nut topping she wanted, and the size she needed all in one breath. In a matter of seconds, Craig placed the assembled dessert down on the counter for her.

She was still holding all of the dirty spoons in her hand, so Craig pointed to the bucket once more and told her that she could throw them away in there if she was finished with them. She smiled and nodded and finally took a step toward the bucket. It sat at the counter, above the various flavors of gelato. She stood on her tippy toes and peered into the bucket. I thought she might rob the already-discarded ones. Instead, she raised her left hand and dropped hers into the bucket. She moved so slowly that I thought she was going to salute them before she departed. Instead, she stepped back in front of the cash register and handed Craig a few bills.

He handed back her change, which she stuffed into her wallet, and he told her, "Have a nice day." But she didn't acknowledge him. As soon as he turned his attention toward me, she jumped between us.

"Can I have a lot of napkins?" she asked. Craig grabbed a fistful of small napkins and slammed them on the counter next to her cup of frozen yogurt with nuts.

The smile that he had greeted the woman with earlier was lost. In a matter of minutes, Craig appeared years older. He aged faster than any President I had seen yet. His face was redder, forehead sweaty. I wasn't ignorant to that feeling. The service industry will age anyone six-times faster than normal.

"I hate these types of customers," I wanted to say to him, staring down the woman as she stuffed her wallet and napkins into her purse. Instead, I stared at the dozen gelato flavors in front of me. I finally had a clear view of the ice cream case, and I searched for my dark chocolate, fearful that it might've been discontinued.

The other eleven flavors were sumptuous, and I craved them all as I searched for my favorite. I found the dark chocolate—right behind the mascarpone Nutella, which sounded amazing. It looked smooth and creamy, blended with dark, sweeping rivers of Nutella. Rather than proclaiming, "One large dark chocolate gelato, please!" as I always had done, I found myself asking for a sample.

Craig handed me a tiny spoonful of the mascarpone Nutella, and it tasted as marvelous as it looked. It would mix perfectly with the dark chocolate. But I continued to scan the other flavors in the case, while I knew I should've been placing my order.

I peered toward the front-right corner of the display case, where the woman before me began her exploration. The Madagascar Vanilla looked tantalizing. It was an off-white, the kind of color you'd paint your linen closet but not a main room. It also had tiny dark beads of crushed vanilla beans speckled throughout so that you'd get two dozen in every spoonful. I needed to fight the urge to ask for another sample, but I could hardly contain myself.

I was turning into the woman before me. I had been to this gelateria more than thirty times, which meant that I had ordered at least thirty-one large dark chocolate gelatos. (One visit I ordered two for myself.) Yet, as I stood at the counter, I was convinced I was missing out. I *needed* to experience more. For the first time at this counter, I questioned myself. There were eleven other flavors for a reason, eleven other Jeep tours I hadn't yet taken. Why was I to so brazenly settle on one?

My dark chocolate gelato was beckoning, though. Its deep chestnut coat looked thick and teeming with velvety saccharinity. It was nothing short of a gently frozen masterpiece. But, then, I couldn't help wondering if the frozen yogurt here was any good.

THE HUNGRY TURTLE

A parent should have a strict ninety seconds to talk about their child, with twenty seconds added on for each additional offspring. There needs to be a time limit, I've determined. Talking about your kid for more than that amount of time in one sitting doesn't make you a good parent. Pride is no substitution for care and attention.

A father of six should be done talking about all of his kids within three minutes and ten seconds. After that time, an alarm should sound, and he'll be carted off by police.

But I just dream.

There is no greater joy than being around my baby son when he babbles, laughs, or finds new ways to escape his playpen like a drunk ninja. It's an unparalleled experience to be near him, to hold him; however, *you have to be there*. Retellings just don't do him justice. That's really the case with *any* subject matter. When I talk about something for more than two minutes straight, even *I* get bored. Wouldn't you rather we discuss all the shades of white paint Benjamin Moore sells now? Their White Dove is just lovely for a sitting room.

I'm happy for you that your children are into sports or are indulging the arts. I just don't have to hear the play by play or see what new doodles made it onto your fridge. Unless they've slide-tackled Cristiano Ronaldo or conquered oil paints, I have to fight to keep my eyelids propped open. If my son pours some acrylics down the side of our discount sofa, sure, I'll take a photo, but I'll think twice about showing you or, God forbid, posting it on Facebook. It's not a Jackson Pollock, for Pete's sake. Kids need at least *some* humility.

I blame my upbringing, although I can't be the only one who was raised this way. The right side of my brain received little parental support while I was growing up. Academics were more important. As long as I was staying out of trouble and getting passing grades, what I did after the school bell rung didn't much matter to my parents. I could write and draw and play music, but whenever I showed my mom and dad something I had created, I was never sure if they had taken their eyes off the TV long enough to see what it was. I didn't think of this as odd back then, and I still don't today. Everyone shows pride in their children differently, I guess.

A coworker, for instance, showed me a video of her daughter one afternoon, even though I didn't ask. Her seven-year-old had written and illustrated an original short story in her free time and made her mom record her reading it. Though I wasn't there, I imagine my coworker, proud of her daughter's intellect and creativity, dropped what she was doing so she could set the stage for the child's performance. The little girl's four pages held together by a single staple would be captured on my coworker's phone in the same manner tourists steal clips of the Pope when he emerges from the Apostolic Palace.

If an interested acquaintance had asked, my mother might have felt obligated, instead of enthused, to share photos or brief videos of my brothers and me. "This is my eldest," she might have said, holding up a photo of me and scouring her mind for something positive to say. "Ignore the gap between his two front teeth—his eyes are *huge*."

My coworker beamed with excitement as she turned the phone just enough so that both of us could watch at the same time. In the video, her daughter introduced herself to the vast audience hidden within the wires of an iPhone 8 and began to read the delicate words scrawled onto green construction paper. The young girl grinned while reading her favorite lines and winced when she mispronounced words. At the end, she slapped the book closed and smiled at the camera. My coworker then replayed the video and repeated every line her daughter read.

While now she is proud of every academic and extracurricular activity her daughter completes, I wondered when she'll find room to criticize the creations of her creation. Isn't it inevitable? I don't even remember the first time my mother did it to me. Maybe it was the first time I wrote a story myself.

By the time I was in third grade, I had written my own original children's picture book entitled *The Hungry Turtle*. The idea for the story was inspired by my voracious red-eared slider and yellow-bellied turtle that I had smuggled into the state. Somewhere in the basement of my childhood home, a rumpled copy of that book still floats on garbage bags stuffed with denim clothing and racecar bedsheets. As the title suggested, the protagonist of this epic suffered a mild starvation. He endures a grueling journey in search of food but comes up empty everywhere he ventures. His problem ultimately is resolved by a long slumber.

I wrote each page of this story on a separate sheet of printer paper, accompanied with spastic illustrations, incorporated an "About the Author" page at the very end, and stapled on a cover I had made with ClipArt. It was a masterpiece, not unlike Picasso's "Old Guitarist" or Stephen King's *Pet Sematary*. I began the process of publicizing my debut book by showing it to the woman who birthed me. It was a tactic that, at the time, I was positive would garner bloated recognition. I was sure I had a bestseller on my hands and would soon become the youngest person ever to seal a deal with a major publication. Penguin Random House, Simon & Schuster, and Scholastic would be falling over each other to get *The Hungry Turtle* to print.

I handed my mother the neat packet while she was tidying up the living room. She stared at the cover, admiring the precision of my stapling abilities down the spine. She flipped through every single page in a matter of seconds and quickly handed it back to me. She simpered and then muttered, "*Niiiiiice*, Patrick," just loud enough for me to hear, but not too vociferous, as if she were afraid the neighbors might hear her compliment her son.

This hadn't been the exact reaction I imagined I'd receive. Maybe I had caught her off guard. She was picking up the scattered innards of Mr. Potato Head from the floor when I had approached her; she wasn't prepared to be handed the next bestselling children's book without an early warning. I decided my mom needed another moment to process the brilliance of my book, and so I waited several more seconds and then asked, "Don't you like it, Mom?"

She didn't return a simple yes or no answer, which the question surely entailed. Instead, she offered similar advice to what an editor might have given me, had I been astute enough to hire one to review the story. My mother looked me directly in the eyes and said, "You know that going to sleep wouldn't make him *full*, right? The turtle would still be hungry after he woke up."

I felt the smile evaporate off my face like an ice pop in the oven. My story had conflict and resolution. Shouldn't that be enough for a "Wow, Patrick! That's impressive! I'm going to call HarperCollins right away!"? She offered nothing of the sort, and I just stood in front of her, probably with my mouth agape.

My mother must have mistaken my stunned silence for confusion when she added, "He'd have to actually eat something to not be hungry anymore." But again I didn't answer and thought intently about crumbling up *The Hungry Turtle* and feeding the pages to my actual pet turtles, who were perpetually ravenous—and supportive.

A stranger might've been concerned about the way my mother blistered her elementary school son. I never thought anything of it. As far as I was concerned, she was being honest. These were words of *constructive* criticism. She didn't sugar coat anything. Oftentimes, she'd tell me exactly what she found wrong with my work; other times, she provided grave yet helpful warnings.

Years before *The Hungry Turtle* was even close to a literary concept in my subconscious, my mom made a habit of playing horror programs on our Mitsubishi television set and calling me to come watch. Quite often, we'd watch *The Langoliers*, a two-part TV miniseries based on the Stephen King novella of the same name. The antagonists of the story, known as Langoliers, were essentially teethy meatballs that would devour time-past. They'd just show up and chomp up the Earth—trees, high-tension wires, and all. My mother and I repeatedly watched the show together, and each time the Langoliers came on screen, she'd get a certain satisfaction in telling me that if I didn't behave, the Langoliers would come after me in my sleep.

My mom made sure that Langoliers weren't the only creatures to ambush me if I acted out. A week before my fifth birthday, my family and I relocated from northern New Jersey to a town in the center of the state. I enjoyed exploring the neighborhood, regularly getting into trouble with old neighbors who didn't want children creasing a single blade of genetically engineered grass on their putting-green front lawns.

Much of the land that became our neighborhood had once been a vast countryside, where farmers and their families had lived, worked, bred, and died. When tucking me in each night, my mom would tell me a story about a farmer with a missing leg, limping around the property on a prosthetic to tend to his cattle. She'd proclaim that the one-legged farmer had lived his entire life on the very grounds where our house now stood. He died in his home nearly one hundred years ago, and though his dwelling was razed shortly after his death, the farmer still haunted this property, looking for his missing leg.

"And," my mom would always add to the end of her tale, "if you don't behave, he's going to take *your* leg when you're asleep."

One sunny Saturday afternoon soon after moving into our new home, my mother felt it necessary to put *Candyman* on the TV after ordering a pizza for lunch. The 1992 horror film may have had a complex storyline, but any themes and artistic motifs were lost to a kindergartner while he nibbled on a slice of pizza and witnessed all the blood and gore and bees. Candyman, who heinously murdered people with his prosthetic metal hook, was only summoned if a person said his name into a mirror three times. However, my mother assured me that he *would* break tradition and come after *me* if I didn't behave.

Before I even reached the first grade, I had an army of horror film monsters waiting for me to misbehave. But though I was not an angel by any stretch, I never sinned badly enough to lose my life to a Langolier or a limb to an angry specter. Santa, who was as real to me as Candyman, only brought me coal once, and the equally legitimate Easter Bunny always remembered to leave milk chocolate eggs by my bedside every year. Consequently, I felt it necessary to never adjust my behavior even slightly; otherwise, I likely would've woken up with a hook through my chest. I was unsure, though, if it would've been the tetanus or the blood loss that would do me in.

I'm not sure at what point I realized these warnings were all fabrications, no more palpable than what news stations produce every day. Embarrassingly, maybe I still believe the ominous cautions.

These were threats, whether true or not. Despite any of this, though, I still consider my mom a saint. I didn't devolve into an unstable adult with an armory in his underground bunker, anticipating the rising of lizard people and the subsequent end of the world. (Hopefully one day I don't regret that . . .)

In between threatening my life and telling me something I made was no good, my mom did practically *everything* for me— and for my brothers and dad, too. She prepared our meals, washed and folded our laundry, cleaned the bathrooms, even rolled the trash out to the curb on the countless evenings when every single one of us forgot about garbage night. If one of us told Mom we liked a particular snack, the pantry would be overflowing with it after her next trip to the grocery store.

I have more fond memories with my mom than bad ones, but that doesn't mean I'll soon forget all the monsters she attempted to sic on me as a kid, nor will I forget the unapologetic criticisms of my works.

I look back on *The Hungry Turtle* as my debut bomb. I continued to write despite how badly it was reviled by the one and only critic to lay eyes on my book. I took her criticisms into account and proceeded to write tales that were much more *logical*. My second short story contained hundreds of magical woodland elves over which my protagonists leaped in order to escape trouble. Other future stories incorporated ghosts and giants and alternate universes and boats made of mattresses. However, I struggled to meet the appeals of my critic and soon abandoned writing. But only temporarily.

I had developed a level of self-doubt that I allowed to dictate my future actions and interests. Most of the writers, artists, and musicians I know have it. It's a mark of the trade. Creative types often wear self-doubt like a tiny tattoo on the inside of the thigh. They're always either afraid to show it or all too excited to spread their legs and display it for anyone in sight. I'm with the former, which has pushed me down different paths throughout my life.

When I turned thirteen, I developed an interest in drawing. I was able to convey messages and emotions in images created with just a pencil. It was writing, but without the words. I started by recreating the logos of my favorite bands: Journey, Led Zeppelin, The Who, Van Halen, Alter Bridge. Quickly becoming bored with repeating the same drawings over and over again, I began redesigning the symbols—making them three-dimensional, encircling them with visible electrical currents, sketching cracks and flaws in the façades. I felt as though I was a part of the next generation of graphic designers. While I was probably only in the initial stages, I might soon go on to design covers for Green Day's next studio album and The Rolling Stones' hundredth record. Mick Jagger and Keith Richards would surely outlive the people who design their album covers and T-shirts. They'd need *me* next.

By the second semester of eighth grade, I carried notebooks filled with more drawings than class notes. I was sure this was a major leap toward my desired career—one I knew I wanted for approximately three days, which might as well have been four years to a thirteen-year-old. My artwork was ready to make its debut. After school one day, I rifled through my backpack to find the notebook with drawings that I was positive would get the most praise.

With my social studies notebook in tow, I approached my mom in the kitchen that evening. She was clearing the clean dinnerware out of the drying rack, humming to herself as she worked. I tapped her shoulder and opened my notebook to my favorite drawing and held it out for her to see.

"Look at this, Mom," I asserted, struggling to hide my smirk. She turned to look at the artwork in my notebook, but her even expression never changed. I flipped through multiple pages, hoping *one* of the drawings might catch her attention.

After several moments, it was clear she didn't know what to say or why I was shoving a social studies notebook—which should've contained notes about the Founding Fathers, not drawings—in her face. So I continued, "Maybe this is what I could do—like, design band logos for a living when I get older."

At this notion, my mom squinted and leaned in closer to the entangled TS for Twisted Sister that I now was holding out for her. I made the letters appear as if they were melting— one of my most creative pieces to date.

My mom shrugged, then shook her head. "Mmm, I don't know. Those people are talented." She took her eyes off my drawing and went back to stacking plates in the cabinet. As if it would clarify her initial reaction and set my self-doubt straight for good, she added, "You would've known by now."

I never wondered if my mom ever talked about my brothers and me to her friends and coworkers. I was sure she didn't. It never bothered me, because even as a teenager I couldn't stand people who talked about their kids all the time.

It wasn't until I was a grown (well, somewhat-grown) man when I learned my mom *was* actually one of those parents. To this day, when I meet her colleagues, they all start the conversations the same way: "Your mom talks so much about you."

She even sells my books to people who she sees on a regular basis—a supposed sure sign that the writing is better than *The*

Hungry Turtle ever was. Her harsh censures and feigned disapproval helped me hone in on my passion (writing) and pushed me to strengthen my craft.

It helped that I never doubted her love for me, although she treaded that line recklessly.

My earliest memory is of my mother singing the refrain to "You Are My Sunshine." She'd croon the lullaby-like tune, disregarding the true, darker meaning of the lyrics, because her loving interpretation purely encapsulated her affection. I listened to her sing to my baby brothers, too. It's just one example of the love my mom has for her sons. Despite knowing better, I can't help but sing "You Are My Sunshine" to my son nearly every day now, too.

I fear that I'll become one of those parents who can't stop talking about his kids, even after ninety seconds have passed and I've been carted off by police. Even still, no matter how amazing I find my current and potential future offspring, I'll make sure to remind them that their shit stinks, just like everyone else's. Oh, and if they misbehave, they'll know exactly who'll be looking for them.

STRANGLING BANANAS

No one rides trains anymore. It's gotten worse since the pandemic, but even commuter lines were declining as work-from-home trends became the norm. Still, there's something to be said about a form of transportation that allows its passengers to crack open beers while the employees look on in jealousy rather than disapproval. As a passenger, I don't judge.

I was by myself on a train ride from Somerville, New Jersey, to New York City about a decade before the pandemic hit. It was a line to Manhattan with a transfer in Newark. My main objective was to get through Ken Kesey's *One Flew Over the Cuckoo's Nest*. That was my go-to reading material when traveling, solely because it fit in my back pocket. Although I ended up enjoying the story, I wasn't able to complete chapter one on my first half-dozen NJ Transit voyages. It was freshman year of college. I had enough assigned books from each class that reading at my leisure became more of a punishment than a hobby. Even when I tried to read a new novel for fun, I always found something to distract me anyway.

On this particular trip, I attempted to restart *Cuckoo's Nest* at Somerville Station, but I was much too fascinated with another individual to even open the book. He was standing about twenty feet farther down the platform, wearing a dark orange down jacket, despite the warm late-September weather. His hair was the same shape and shade of brown as a meatball. With both his hands, he gripped a noticeably bruised banana like a tennis racket.

I often judge people who stare, but today I was the ogler. I knew if I looked away even for a second, he would do something interesting with that banana. I didn't know what I wanted him to do with it though—whack a pedestrian, throw it at the train—but I would've been devastated, after sixteen minutes of staring at this man, if I witnessed him simply peel and eat it. The least he could do was scarf down the entire fruit, rind and all. Maybe then I wouldn't be too upset.

When our train arrived and the doors opened, the man clutched the banana tighter in his fists. The rind split, and the insides seeped out like the mushy guts of a fallen gladiator. He seemed to be startled by the train's arrival, as if he had no idea there'd be a train coming, at the train station, directly on the tracks. After two beats, he took one slow step forward before sprinting inside as he licked his fingers, the banana still in his vice grip.

I entered the train one car behind him. I was curious where he ended up, or if he just ran back out of the train, but I was more concerned with finding a peaceful spot where I could read. The quiet cars are always impossible to find, unless, of course, you travel with a group of friends who only want to discuss sports and which porn-themed convention was their favorite. In those instances, the groups gravitate to the quiet cars. Transit workers eventually ask these groups to leave, but only after their conversations are no longer interesting.

The train took off immediately after I stepped on. I stumbled through several cars before settling on a seat behind a brunette who was involved with a paperback. She lay the book across her lap as she leaned against the window, letting the sun freely peek in on the narrative. I threw my backpack on the aisle seat next to me and hunted for the ticket I had just bought. If you ever wanted to lose a small piece of paper, you could give it to me. You'd never see it again. Movie tickets, Polaroids, hate notes—I lose them all, and completely by accident.

The conductor made his way down the railcar and stopped next to my seat as I continued mining my backpack. The frown he brandished embraced the bottom half of his face, as if he were irritated with me for vandalizing his house rather than wasting his time. He tapped his foot and shouted down the aisle, "Tickets out!" as he stuck out his hand, showing me his palm.

After I finally found the ticket in the left-front pocket of my jeans, he snatched it out of my hand, methodically punctured it with his special hole puncher, and handed it back.

When he moved onto the next unsuspecting passenger, I pulled *Cuckoo's Nest* out of my back pocket but kept my eye on the reflection of the woman in front of me. I was a single college freshman majoring in English, and I was enamored by the sight of a woman, looking about my age, whose phone was nowhere to be found while her book was prominently displayed. Her pages turned with fury. Every now and then, she'd lick her red lips and pull the book closer to her nose before relaxing it back on her lap.

"You should ask her out," my high-school friend Spencer would say every time I expressed even the slightest interest in a girl. I didn't even have to say someone was attractive for him to play Cupid. If I even looked in the general direction of a female—including a teacher or the school's old Polish-speaking janitor—he'd nudge my shoulder and smirk. I imagined he'd do the same to me now.

"Just go up to her and ask her out on a date, dude," he used to direct. "The worst she could say is no."

"Do you even go to this school?" I would ask him. "The *best* she could say is no. The worst she could say is I'm a scrawny, little pathetic wannabe werewolf-looking freak who'll never get a date as long as he lives."

"You're so paranoid."

I knew I wasn't going to ask this woman out. I didn't even want to talk to her. I couldn't just plop myself down in the empty seat next to her and say, "This train gets crowded the closer we get to the city. We're better off sitting together now before some weirdo does instead." I wasn't—and still am not—

in any way suave and wouldn't have been able to stop talking once I started. I might've complimented her choice of lipstick, so then what right did I have to call someone *else* a weirdo? Plus, I didn't know if I had any real interest in her or if I was just attracted to her book. I constantly tried to identify what she was reading but couldn't get a single glimpse of the cover.

I decided against engaging her and instead started the first chapter of *Cuckoo's Nest* by the time our train reached the next stop.

When we halted two stops later at the Bound Brook station, I looked out my window. A group of eight high-school boys struggled to find the proper entrance to the train. They looked like a family of silver dollar fish. When the leader walked forward, the entire group moved forward; when the leader turned right, the entire group turned right. They soon made their way aboard and found themselves in my car, scattered about several rows of seats.

"Do you know how long the ride is?" one asked.

"About an hour," another answered. "Make sure you have your tickets out." Though I felt compelled to tease them, this guy was one step ahead of me, and he didn't even know it.

"I need to use the bathroom," another one of them announced. "Is there a bathroom on the train? Where's the bathroom?"

The group never let a single moment pass silently. It was like a chicken coop. They had the noise and odor levels down pat. They discussed a number of comprehensive topics at a speed I had trouble keeping up with. I read and reread each sentence of an entire page before I closed my book and let it balance on my leg. As captivating as I had found the beginning of *Cuckoo's Nest*, any story pales in comparison to teenage conversations about what *BuzzFeed* deems "New York City hotspots," dying cell phone batteries, and how cruel Janine had been to Brad recently. Obviously, it didn't take long for me to realize that I wasn't in the quiet car, and I had nearly every single passenger to remind me of that.

When the train stopped at the Westfield station, a man in green-ish jeans and a brown sweatshirt entered my car. It was a striking ensemble. I figured his clothes were once brighter in color but had soured over time. He held his cell phone like a fine glass of merlot, despite the aggravating barking that shot out of it.

By the early twenty-first century, many Americans had decided that their conversations were so crucial to the public that they utilized the speaker phone option on their mobile devices while in the company of complete strangers. This man was one of them.

"You cannot be late tonight, *Al*!" the high-pitched voice inside the phone shouted with an accent that made it sound like she was saying "Ale." When the man opened his mouth to respond, the voice continued. "I'm serious, Al! You cannot be late again tonight!"

The man—Al, I presumed—sat in the row of seats across the aisle from me. His eyes were closed, head tilted back, and he held his phone farther away from his face with every passing remark from the caller on the other line. Then, when Al decided the phone was too far away from him, he pulled it right back up to his face, as if he were sniffing the buttons. In that moment, I felt his pain. The voice continued to harass my new buddy Al, and he didn't even bother to howl back. He kept his eyes closed and face even. When the shrill voice slowed, Al opened his eyes, determined not to miss his opportunity to speak. "I hope you're listening to me, Al," the voice called out. "Al . . . I'm serious . . ."

Seeing his window, Al sat up and cleared his throat, brought the phone even closer to his mouth, and said, "Honey . . . I have no intention of going." Then he hit a button on the device and stuffed it into his pocket.

Inspired by Al, the man sitting behind him dialed someone on his own cell phone and began talking about remodeling his colonial in Boonton. He told the person on the other end of the line that he preferred hardwood floors. "Every room," he said. "I want hardwood in *every* room. Hardwood on the walls too, if I can." As is common in rooms with hardwood flooring, this man mentioned purchasing high-end area rugs, repeatedly referring to them as "areola rugs." I counted six times, but he may have said it more. I considered correcting him, for the sake of his dignity, but would I then have had to explain what an areola actually is? I wasn't trained, or even educated, for that. Instead, I chuckled, and the man turned and noticed me looking at him. I shot my eyes back down to the closed book on my lap and picked it up, trying to find where I had left off. After a few seconds of flipping through pages, I glanced in Al's direction. His body was facing the window, shoulder on the seat, and his head was against the backrest.

I focused my attention back on the passenger in front of me. She now was tilted forward, her face closer to the book in her lap, probably putting all of her energy into reading despite all the racket that surrounded her. When the train's robotic voice announced that we were approaching Newark Penn Station, our transfer point, the woman folded the book closed across her lap, and in the hazy reflection I caught the cover of what she had been reading. The background was dark gray with shades of blue and silver that blended together in a ghostly coil. I had seen it someplace before, but I wasn't sure where. When the woman shifted in her seat, moving the novel closer to the window, I was able to read it more clearly. The reflected letters read *50 Shades of Grey*.

I had heard of this book. The professor in one of my composition courses had brought it up when a student asked about alternatives to traditional publishing. This originally was a self-published novel that was picking up steam for only one reason: it was porn. Poorly written porn, from what I understood. My professor and several students spent half the class berating and criticizing the book and seemingly everything about it. As far as I knew, it wasn't real literature and anyone who read it didn't actually *read*.

I gasped. The train grinded to a halt, making sure to jolt forward one more time before rocking back to a rest. The woman in front of me stood up, and I couldn't help but look at her and assess her features. Her fiery lips somehow looked paler than they'd been in the reflection, her skin pasty. All the vibrancy seemed to drain from her like bleach down a toilet bowl. What I thought I had been seeing in the reflection of that dirty polycarbonate window was merely a mirage, not the oasis I had hoped for. I blamed it on her novel of choice. Had she been reading *Misery* or *Slaughterhouse-Five* or *The Great Gatsby*, I wondered if I would've reacted differently. I continued to stare at her anyway for some reason, and I couldn't imagine I had the most pleasant expression on my face, but still she turned in my direction and smiled at me. I didn't smile back and hopped down from my seat and hurried to the exit of the railcar, unsure if I was disappointed or confused.

As I walked to the end of the car, ready to fling my body out of the locomotive as soon as the doors opened, I noticed a cream-colored mush on the floor by my exit. It was as grainy as applesauce but lighter in color. Instantly, I knew it was from the banana strangler I had seen at Somerville Station. Who else could have been responsible? The guy probably exited through this car, his hand still slick with banana innards. He must have lost some on his way off the train.

As it turned out, he was the most interesting part of this train ride. All of the others showed their hand at their first opportunity, but he maintained a veil of mystery. It somehow was a fitting way to begin a trip to Manhattan. I couldn't understand why he had done it, though. Maybe he purposely dropped some of his uneaten banana by the exit so that a pas-senger would slip and fall. Was it a good sign then that I caught this trap before I succumbed to it? Thinking of what kind of man destroys a ripe banana in public in broad daylight, I won-dered if maybe this was just his way of sharing.

FORTY

Servers and bartenders follow an unwritten rule whenever guests leave phone numbers on credit card receipts: they cannot keep the tip unless they intend to call or text the guest. I find this ludicrous, because I believe gratuity in those cases to be like down payments on a potential venture, and sometimes investments fall through. That's the risk of investing in today's market and why so many singles have stuck with free and cost-effective options like Tinder, Bumble, and Match.com. Hell, I'd try Craigslist before ever leaving a fat tip alongside my phone number at an American eatery.

I just wasn't familiar with this side of the restaurant business. When I started waiting tables, I never expected to find ten digits jotted on a receipt or napkin and kissed by red lips, like something out of a Bogart film. Things like that just didn't happen to me.

Freshman year of college, I got a job hosting before soon

advancing to serving. I was a full-time student and put in even more hours working every week. I didn't have *time* to care about how I was viewed by anyone else. It wasn't like in middle school or high school, where I cared what others thought of what I said and did. I believed that their being judgmental and my being self-conscious were completely normal and even required of human beings. I didn't like the feeling of being ridiculed when I spilled a little carton of milk in the cafeteria or said the word "second" funny in class. It's easier, if not foolproof, for kids with heightened humility to stay quiet and out of sight, especially when we had more faults than a city roadway.

By thirteen years old, I was able to grow a healthy beard. I know now that wasn't a "fault" by any stretch, but teenagers can find anything to be embarrassed by. Aside from my upper lip, where the uneven facial hair refused to connect with the scruff on my cheeks, I'd have a werewolf-caliber coat of fur on my mug if I didn't shave for a few days. Had I not employed the frequent use of a razor and shaving cream, I'd be subject to apprehension by animal control every day at school. I was unsure if faculty would view me as a chimpanzee or an unwashed Komondor, but I was positive that I would not be welcome in a classroom. Pets weren't allowed in school, and as far as I knew, you couldn't register a dog for eighth grade. At least not in New Jersey.

During middle school and high school, I was never mistaken for a teacher. Perhaps if I dressed a little more formally, that slipup might have occurred, but I dressed as if I were rebelling against nuns at a Catholic school. So with my stone-washed jeans and hard-rock-themed T-shirts a size too big, no one was going to mistake me for someone who graduated college. On top of that, I stopped growing when I was around thirteen, and I stayed relatively petite. You could lose me in an overgrown field. If I was going to be mistaken for anyone in school, it'd be the substitute teacher who was a stunt double for child actors.

Much of my senior year of high school was spent down the art wing. I discovered film and cartooning a year or so before and didn't care about much else. The art wing was a safe space for the nerdy outcasts, watery eyes buried in sketchbooks, hands stained with red and black paint. It was both cool and uncool to be there, but none of us cared.

One day toward the end of my senior year, I was walking down that long hallway, a bright yellow Strathmore sketchbook tucked under my arm. Two female students turned the corner at the opposite end of the hallway and headed in my direction. I could hardly make out their features, and the only thing that was clear to me was that one had dark brown hair and the other was blonde. There were no other students around, and the hall was silent, but still neither girl made any attempt to lower her voice, even as they spoke about me. I heard, "He's cute," and as they got closer, I looked at them and smiled. Their features were clearer now, but they still didn't look familiar.

Although my grade consisted of roughly six hundred students, I recognized most of them. These two looked just a tad too young to be seniors. At the time, twelfth graders seemed to be more refined than even eleventh graders. But it was really just cockiness. We had just undergone what felt like a lifetime of public schooling and were on our way to "the real world," as we referred to post-high-school life—even though "the real world" isn't a place you knowingly enter; it's something that devours your lifeboat and drags you into the salty abyss like Jaws. The independence in the air of senior year is an illusion, a hallucinogen. It helps you act more like a tool, but not the useful kind. It even changes the way you walk, a little bit slower, taking in the hallways and the windows, as if you won't still be living in town for the next four, five, ten years.

The two girls I was passing in the hallway of the art wing didn't come off this way. I pegged them as either sophomores or juniors. The one with the straight brown hair wore thin-rimmed glasses, and as she smiled back at me, I saw her teeth were wired with braces. The other had deliberately wavy hair, like strips of bacon, and a small mole below her right eye. She returned no type of smile, only making eye contact with me for a second before spinning her head toward her friend and saying, "Ew, he looks like he's forty."

I snickered, even though I didn't find it funny. I didn't think she was wrong, though. I was never a fan of my genes. Just like every other teenager on the planet, I was self-conscious and blamed my DNA, because I couldn't take any of the responsibility for that. I didn't erupt like a Chia Pet by the sheer force of my own willpower. I didn't fertilize my cheeks for years so that they'd become more fruitful than a pumpkin patch in October. None of this was my own doing. I figured: I have no control over my hair, size, or features—if any of that is undesirable, that's not my fault; it's my parents', or grandparents', or great-grandparents', or great-great-grandparents'. But not mine. When I didn't do my homework or when I failed a vocabulary quiz, you could've blamed those shortcomings on me. But when I look nearly three-times my age, that's genetics. Thanks a lot, Great-Great-Grandad Alfredo.

After the girl made that remark, I nearly turned around to shout, "It's not my fault!" That wouldn't have made the situation better. I probably would've felt even more embarrassed. I thought better of shouting anything and instead kept walking and contemplated whether or not that was the lowest part of my senior year. At the moment, it was a wonder to me why I wasn't shot at like that more often than a dart board. The only thing saving me from daily ridicule was that other guys in my school were jealous of my ability to grow a thick beard. They frequently felt the need to tell me.

"Why don't you grow out your beard?" my classmate, Dylan, once asked me in the middle of a music lesson. I chuckled, and he replied, "No, seriously. I wish I had facial hair like that." Dylan nodded while staring at my cheeks. Then his eyes drifted down to my arms, which had as much fur as a husky with mites, and he added, "I just want your facial hair though, not your arms." He touched the back of one of my forearms with his index finger. "Do you lose things in there?"

I looked down at my arm and petted it like a kitten. "All the time," I told him. "Stuff's always falling out of 'em in the shower."

When I became a waiter, one of my concerns was that ornery guests might return food with hairs in it, accusing me of plucking a strand from my arm and garnishing the dish with it. I had plenty to spare, so I thought this was a probability. It never happened, but I continued to worry, especially when groups of girls would visit and gawk at my arms as I placed their berry salads and veggie wraps in front of them. They could've just been ogling their food, but I thought for sure they were looking for excuses to joke and giggle as soon as my back was turned.

A couple years into serving, with this specific concern still as prominent as it was on my first day, I waited on a group of four girls. But they weren't girls; they were more than likely freshmen or sophomores in college. At this age, you're just about adults. "Girls" and "boys" were left in the gymnasium after they tossed their caps into the air. Three of the women at this table were unfamiliar to me, but I recognized the blonde with the bacon-style hair and tiny mole under her eye. I wasn't sure if she recognized me, but since she smiled every time I approached the table, I doubted she remembered I was the forty-year-old with a sketchbook roaming the high school art wing a few years before.

I never tainted anyone's meal while working in a restaurant, though I regularly wanted to. Oddly, however, I had no desire to do anything ill-advised to her food or drink. Maybe it was because I felt that I had matured since high school—that payback would never satisfy me then the way it might have three years prior. Or perhaps it was because the girl was trying so hard to be nice to me that I would've felt guilty if I poured Tabasco sauce into her Diet Pepsi. She repeatedly said please and thank you as if someone was pulling a string on her back, causing her to blurt it out every time I visited the table. And she didn't miss the opportunity to compliment my speed and attentiveness. I was intentionally *slow* and *inattentive* with her table, but I still accepted the compliment as if I were some remarkable servant.

"Thank you so much," she said with a grin when I handed her a refill ten minutes after she asked for it. "You have such lovely green eyes," she added, and I heard her friends giggle as I walked away without acknowledging her.

When the four women finished their dinner, I brought them their separate checks. They all paid with credit cards, and as I returned the cards and receipts, the blonde's smile and eyes widened, and she thanked me for my "excellent service," as she described it. I ignored her, bid the guests farewell, and walked toward the kitchen at the other end of the restaurant. Behind my back, I heard the blonde mutter something low, followed by giggling.

It meant little to me then. I wasn't a boy anymore, or at least that's what I told myself. Graduating from high school didn't automatically spring me into adulthood; it just catapulted me into some of the grime and crud associated with it. I might have gone from being a boy to a man, but I hardly felt as though

I was a mature, capable "adult" in reality. I was just a kid who shaved more than he used to. But I figured if I made myself believe that I was an adult, even if just for a little while, I might be able to make myself act like one, too.

I wondered if the blond woman told her friends that I looked seventy now, that I aged ten years every year since she last saw me. I snickered again, just as I had done three years before, but this time it was because I thought it was funny. I didn't find the humor in it last time, because I had cared what people thought of me then. Not just any "people," though— people I didn't even know.

I wasn't sure if I actually looked forty, but I intended to *act* like it. Ridicule didn't have the same effect on me as it did when I was thirteen or even seventeen. Maybe I just didn't have the juvenile energy to be anything but apathetic, but I was hopeful that the culprit was simply newfound maturity.

When the four young ladies walked out of the restaurant, I ventured back toward their table. All I needed were their credit card slips so that I could enter their tips, if any, into the computer and be one table closer to finishing my shift.

I had removed most of the dirty plates and glasses before they left, so the table was particularly empty when I came back to pick up the credit card receipts. They were stacked in the center of the table, with a curious one on top. The amount for the top bill was about twenty-five dollars, and a five-dollar tip would have sufficed. But the owner of this receipt gave me more than triple that, bringing her total to an even forty dollars. Below the total, she signed her name beside a message scrawled with a runny blue pen: *Thank you again for your excellent service!* The second letter *i* was dotted with a heart, and below the message was a phone number and a note adding *(I'm the blond one).*

I was in unfamiliar territory. No one had ever left me a number before, and unsurprisingly, no one ever left me a phone number again. Aside from the occasional *Thank you*, people rarely scribbled more than a tip and their signature on a credit card receipt, and sometimes they didn't even do *that* much. So I was surprised to see ten uniform digits at the bottom of the receipt, especially from someone who saw me and exclaimed "ew" just a few years before.

After collecting a guest's credit card receipt, servers are required to enter the gratuity amount into the computer, and this is added to what we take home at the end of the night. I carried the four receipts over to one of the computers in the corner of the restaurant and entered the other three tips into the system. They were between fifteen and twenty percent of their respective bills, but this fourth one—the one with the phone number—was a sixty-percent tip. A substantial amount.

I was certain from the moment I saw the phone number that I had no intention of calling her. I was dating a coworker, who is now my wife, but even if I hadn't been, I had lost all interest in this woman the moment she passed me in the school hallway three years before. (Huh, maybe I *don't* let things go.)

I had a different dilemma, though, as I stood at the computer. I was unsure if I could enter that tip. As I had learned from servers who regularly received phone numbers—or at least *claimed* to have regularly received them—you shouldn't keep a large credit card tip if you don't intend to call the number that was left for you. (If someone leaves a phone number for you but also leaves a small tip, that's a different story.)

There's perhaps much debate about the ethics here, as many service workers say that since you don't show any interest in the person, you also shouldn't show any interest in their money either. But if she insulted me several years prior and I still thought about it, wouldn't I have then been entitled to the large tip as a compensatory sum, even if I wasn't ever going to contact her? I pondered this for several minutes at the computer that night, neglecting the two tables I was still taking care of.

I opened the screen to enter her tip, ready to hit the number zero, when I started to rub my scruff. I didn't shave that morning, and the short layer of facial hair that covered my cheeks like coal was thick and coarse.

I looked down at the total amount she had written on the credit card receipt. It was an even forty. I hadn't made the connection earlier, but that was the age she said I looked when I passed her in the hallway a few years ago. I was unsure now if this was a genuine tip or a creative way to ridicule me. Whatever it was, I was impressed.

I scratched the scruff on my cheeks some more and noticed the small bald spots that made it uneven. I found it hard to believe that many forty-year-olds had facial hair as jagged as mine. That should be sufficient enough proof that I was not middle aged. Perhaps that wasn't what made me look older, though. At the time, I hadn't identified any wrinkles on my face or thinning of my hair. I could pick out a couple white hairs on my head, but I had to actively search in the mirror to find them. Yet, I couldn't help but imagine what qualities might have made me appear twice as old as I was.

I tried, even for that short moment leaned up against the computer, to act like an adult, to shake it off. I wanted to ignore the voice in my head that reminded me that I missed my opportunity three years ago to tell her off, to tell her how great it is to look much older than I am, to tell her that I don't even get carded at the bar. (I'd leave out the part about how I only ordered sodas.)

Despite all of my thoughts, all my ideas to get revenge, I continued to stand at the computer for a while that night, just scratching at the unshaven scruff on my face. I wondered if I really did mature since my teenage years, or if I'm still that same kid who could grow a wicked beard by thirteen years old.

EVERYTHING FALLS

My dad had a theory when I was growing up that my mom used to booby trap the kitchen cabinets. He said she did it to the pantry and the refrigerator, too. My mother would be in and out of those spaces all day long without a hiccup, but once my dad entered the pantry in search of a snack, some loose item would plummet to the ground. It'd crash on the floor with a clatter that echoed throughout the entire house, nearly sending my father into a fit of panic. According to him, all he had to do was open a door and a trap would trigger. Without fail, something would fall out of the enclosure as if it were trying to escape. Whether it was a big or small object, heavy or light, my dad would turn the unfortunate experience into an off-Broadway production. Soon enough, our neighbors would hear as he narrated the crisis.

"Wow, Gina," he'd say to my mom, his baritone voice booming as he'd throw his hands into the air. "Everything falls in this house. I came in here for a Devil Dog, and stuff starts flying off the shelves." He'd reach to the ground to pick up whatever had fallen, a spatula or granola bar. "I didn't even *touch* anything!" He'd put it somewhere it didn't belong, like in between boxes of batteries or on top of a jug of iced-tea mix. "You really got this closet set up like a trap. I can't even open the door without being ambushed."

The truth is that the pantry was always overfilled. It was maintained mostly as an additional storage space for non-edible items. We kept unused promotional water bottles from local businesses stacked toward the bottom, joined by unopened gift boxes and assorted holiday decorations. There were sewing tools in round cookie tins, rolls of scotch tape balanced on cereal boxes, and bags of expired protein powder blocking containers filled with Italian-made pens. When I was still in school, we kept old photo albums underneath a basket filled with tortilla chips and hot dog rolls. If one dug deep enough, he was likely to discover He-Man action figures fused to a sticky bag of stale marshmallows.

At some point, my mother purchased a closet organizer—either from the dollar store or an estate sale—and hung it on the inside of the pantry door. This allowed even more storage for things like peanut butter, Nutella, maple syrup, honey, vitamins, Tylenol, and more rolls of scotch tape. The rack didn't always lie flush against the back of the pantry door, and if you opened it just quickly enough, you could cause Mrs. Butterworth to slip behind the rack and tumble to the floor. My dad classified this as a booby trap, but I always believed it to be a combination of cheap technology and operator error. You didn't have to be Indiana Jones to drift in and out of our kitchen without falling victim to gravity, but you at least had to train for it.

On nights when my parents were binge watching reruns of *Naked and Afraid* in the next room, I'd have to slip quietly into the kitchen if I wanted to make myself an ice cream sundae. I was a music director conducting an orchestra, my left and right hands clearly not communicating but still getting the job done. One hand would open the freezer at the exact same time the other would open the fridge. I'd grab the carton of ice cream while carefully lifting the chocolate syrup from behind an oversized jar of mayonnaise. Then I'd close both doors simultaneously, minimizing the decibels as much as possible. No matter how hard I tried, it was never enough. I would've failed out of ninja academy; I just know it.

"What did he say?" I'd hear my mom ask in the middle of an episode.

"I don't know. I can't hear the TV," my dad would answer. "Your son is rearranging the furniture in there."

In reality, I had only touched one glass bowl. But I couldn't put it down softly enough on the Formica countertop so that it wouldn't even clink. Gravity just doesn't work that way.

Legend has it that Sir Isaac Newton was immeasurably elated when he was sitting under an apple tree in a park and one of the spherical fruits dropped down and plunked him on the head. I learned in the fourth grade that this was how gravity was discovered, but I've never fact checked the tale. I believe it, however. And I imagine that had it been my father under the apple tree that day, the discovery of gravity would've been blamed on my mother. Rather than calling it "gravity," we instead would refer to this phenomenon as "Gina's hijinks."

Something was always someone else's fault in my house. It's why I am the way I am today, I suppose. I'm happy to blame a politician whenever my taxes increase (every year) or a driver when a car cuts me off on the highway. I couldn't run a fantasy football league, let alone a state or country, but I'll resolve to blame the ones who do. My childhood informed my adulthood, and if there's one thing I'm sure of, it—whatever *it* is—is not my fault. In fact, growing up, I usually *knew* who was responsible for most of my dilemmas: the person who birthed me.

My mom didn't often argue her innocence when a box of oatmeal would somersault out of the pantry or a container of blueberries would swan dive out of the fridge. All the males in our household had been hit with falling debris at some point or another. It couldn't have been an accident *every* time. If I had spent decades cleaning up after messy people, I might get a certain satisfaction in planting playful traps in various inconspicuous locations.

The evidence supporting my theory, though, doesn't hang together consistently or rationally. The only fact I've actually discovered is that my mother would try to distract my brothers and me whenever we'd accuse her of some maternal misconduct. Whenever we confronted her with accusations, all she would do was ask us, "What do you want for dinner?" Then we'd mindlessly sweep up the dropped cereal and contemplate what we wanted for our next meal. Completely sidetracked.

My mom also incorrectly used words of which she knew the definitions. She did this to divert my attention when I'd start complaining to her, because that was the quickest way to get me to quit my griping. I'd then take it upon myself to clarify what she meant, as if I were some sort of walking dictionary-thesaurus hybrid. Today, this is called "mansplaining," but back then it should've been considered "teensplaining," since all teenagers on the planet believe they are smarter and wiser than their parents, despite having less education and a fraction of the life and work experience. (Three-year-olds are like this, too. They're the teens of toddlers.) Instead of being offended by it, though, my mother manipulated my brothers and me into teensplaining everything so that she didn't have to listen to us whine and complain instead.

On one occasion when I opened the pantry door and a tube of dried parsley rolled off a package of English muffins and crashed into my big toe, my mother told me, "I keep dried parsley for emergencies." Pompously, I felt the need to clarify her incorrect usage of the term "emergencies."

I lifted the cylindrical container from the kitchen floor and stared at it for a few moments before responding. It was about three-quarters of the way filled with green specks. It looked no different from any other dried herb I'd seen, but I wondered if there really were emergencies that required parsley. Maybe some people kept freeze-dried forms of the plant in the bottom drawer of their end tables, easily accessible in the event a burglar entered the home at night. Then they'd be prepared to creep downstairs to confront the home invader with a bag of dried parsley, or maybe a cylindrical container of the herb like this one. You could blow it into someone's eyes and just about blind them, I suppose. Me, I'd rather be shot in the leg.

More likely, though, my mother kept the dried parsley in case one of her sons were kidnapped. Had the captor demanded a ransom of five ounces of the stuff *immediately*, my mother would have had us home before the kidnapper rounded the corner. She'd swap the product for us right away, because, after all, this was the emergency she was waiting for. In such a case, she would be nothing short of a hero, and I'd have been a fool to insist that one *didn't* keep dried parsley for emergencies.

Without saying a word, I handed the bottle to my mother. She tucked it away behind a carton of Morton salt in a cabinet next to the stove, far from the pantry.

I finally figured that my mother must have kept dried parsley for her elaborate booby traps. I imagined that once I left the kitchen, she'd balance the bottle on the edge of a box of stovetop stuffing before closing the pantry door. Then, when my father was in search of a Devil Dog, he'd open the door and the plastic bottle would plummet to the floor like an apple in autumn, sending my father into another momentary tirade.

As he had pantomimed, those times constituted emergencies. No one was in immediate danger, nor was anyone on the verge of collapse, but the peace was disturbed. Elsewhere, residents called the police when such crimes were committed in their neighborhoods, didn't they? It counted for something.

EVERYTHING FALLS

Once again, I was convinced that it wasn't *my* fault a bottle of hot sauce fell out of the fridge and cracked on the linoleum. Neither was it gravity's fault that everything falls.

A MIDSUMMER NIGHT'S EXPO

Christine spent the entire calendar year 2019 documenting her schedule in a small hardcover planner. Doctor appointments, lunch dates, solar eclipses—everything short of tracking her period was scribbled in that ledger. I had gotten it for her for Christmas 2018. In fact, I get her one every year for no other reasons than it's cheap and she likes it.

This particular one had a William Shakespeare quote on the cover—instead of cartoon puppies or neon flowers, as most had. It read, *And though she be but little, she is fierce.* It's from his comedy *A Midsummer Night's Dream*. In the play, one woman says that line about another, and although originally the phrase may have been intended as an insult—or maybe a backhanded compliment—the passing of more than four hundred years has turned it into a proverb. It's motivational now and printed on shirts, mugs, canvases, and planners. Christine loved it and used the book at every opportunity.

In July 2's box she wrote, *Free burgers with Pat*, because on that date I had lured her to Lahaska, Pennsylvania, where we had had our first date seven years before. In 2019, I told her that I had a voucher for free burgers that was expiring that random Tuesday evening. The ploy was so I could catch her off guard; the real plan was a proposal.

Christine said yes that evening, and after we embraced, I broke the bad news to her: there were no free burgers. Instead, we paid full price for our meals at the same restaurant where we had our first date. The next day, I told her about an upcoming bridal show, and she scrawled that into her planner, too. She wanted to go together, and I begrudgingly agreed.

"I meant *you* should go," I thought about telling her. "I'll hang back at home and relax. Let me know if there's anything good."

The event was one night only and three hours long, so I didn't put up a fight. I didn't think that would've been a strong way to start off an engagement.

We each drove straight from work to the convention center, where the event was being held. The rain was pounding and flooding parts of the state, and many of the bridal show vendors were running late or not showing up at all. Most of the ones who were there already had not yet finished setting up by the time we arrived. Some were emptying boxes of gaudy, ornate junk onto their tables—enormous floral arrangements, Elizabethan era candlesticks, vases filled with marbles and water.

Most of these items were taller than us, but to be fair, we're on the shorter end of the spectrum, with koalas and child actors.

I was curious what types of people wanted items like these at their wedding. Perhaps they were going for more of a Beverly Hills yard-sale-type aesthetic. Then again, if I had it my way, I would've held my wedding reception in the middle of an open field surrounded by my favorite food trucks, so maybe I shouldn't judge others. The only thing keeping me from fighting for a food truck reception was the fact that I knew it'd rain on my wedding day. It usually rains when I need to be outside. I've learned to adapt, mostly by always staying in.

Christine and I were admiring a fishbowl, which, for some reason, displayed wedding rings, when a tuxedo vendor snuck up behind us. "Good evening! How are you? My name is Don," the gentleman said, all in one breath. His hair was an orange tumbleweed atop his head. His suit was fresh and cleanly pressed and a dazzling shade of blue, like toilet bowl cleaner. He was holding a clipboard, and I immediately knew where this was going.

"You must be the lucky groom," he said to me, smiling. "Do you know where you'll be getting your suit or tuxedo from?" Before I had an opportunity to shake my head, he pulled me over to his table, saying he wanted to show me everything they offered. He pointed to a stack of Hershey's chocolate bars wrapped in golden coupons. "For you, with this coupon—just for signing up with us today and scheduling an appointment to meet at one of our stores—we'll give you seventy dollars off your entire purchase for your best man and groomsmen, and *your* tux is completely free. How many men will be in your party? It doesn't matter. As long as you have six. Here, fill out this form." He handed me his clipboard. "Just write six. You don't need to know anything else. You don't need to know what color you want, what type of tux or suit you want. Nothing. Just come in for your appointment, and you'll get the seventy dollars off if you decide to work with us. If you don't, that's okay. We want you to shop around and get the suit that's best for you. But if you do pick us, you'll get that big discount—that seventy dollars off. Usually, we only give a discount of forty-five dollars, but since you're scheduling an appointment with us today, I'll give you seventy off."

I already owned the suit I planned to be buried in, but if I didn't, I would've been inclined to go with his store and get seventy dollars off. I felt the urge then to ask him if this discount applied to cadavers as well, but I suppressed it. I didn't think he'd take me seriously.

I filled out the form he had handed me. One of the shops was near my house, and maybe with seventy dollars off *and* my tux free, it would turn out to be a reasonable cost. He was giving me seventy dollars off, he told me. And for a second, I might've been foolish enough to believe I'd be the only person getting that excellent deal. Oh! And did I mention he was going to give me seventy dollars off . . .?

I scheduled an appointment to meet with him the following week and gave the form back. Then he handed Christine and me the chocolate bars, immediately becoming my favorite person at the event. I peeled the coupon off the wrapper. "It's for the seventy-dollars-off deal," the man reminded me. "The guys at our company did it based on the *Willy Wonka and the Chocolate Factory* movie. I had never seen it before. Then I watched it." He shrugged.

Christine chuckled and wished him a good night, and finally I began to feel free as we increased the distance between us and the tux guy. But before we could take more than a couple steps, a woman from a fitness company intercepted us and forced us to her table. I felt like I was being passed off like a baton in a relay race.

The woman was wearing a neon-orange sweat suit with a matching orange headband. The clothes were unblemished, as if she had just taken them off the rack that afternoon. She wasn't very talkative, but still the graphic-heavy poster board behind her table somehow told me less than she did about what she was peddling. What I gathered was that this particular business scheme was directed toward a female market. It used fitness and nutrition to prepare brides and their bridal parties for the big day—the "big day" being the five-hour block during one night when the newly married couple and all of their guests attempt to eat double their body weight in food. This company assured us that we needed preparation for that.

Christine had already begun digging into her chocolate bar as the entrepreneur so passionately spoke about the importance of a balanced diet, void of empty calories and saturated fats. We laughed, but the woman found little of the interaction amusing. She just wanted our information and commitment to visit one of their facilities before she'd let us go—you know, your typical hostage situation. Christine told her no thank you, and the two of us turned to roam the rest of the bridal show—cattle off to the slaughter house.

We walked out of the first room and down a short hallway to a space quadruple the size of the first. This area was filled with entertainment companies, photographers, videographers, all-inclusive vacation agencies, and other businesses. A woman helped us set up our registry with Bed, Bath & Beyond, while another gave us chocolate chip cookies. It was a positive environment, until you learned that the entertainment and vacation vendors were as volatile as African cichlids. Maybe they wanted you to have a good time at your wedding—I couldn't argue that—but they mostly just wanted your money. This bridal show was supposed to be a sampling of what options were out there for brides and grooms. We went in thinking we could dip our toes in the water, maybe wade a bit in the tide. But all of the DJs and MCs in attendance pulled us to their massive, expensive displays before we could escape back to our lifeboat.

The entertainment companies at the bridal show were able to provide us with tons of information and an overview of their packages, most of which we weren't interested in, or at least *I* wasn't.

"Were you guys looking to get a photo booth at your wedding?" one DJ asked us.

"No," I told him.

"How about an extra, customized lighting package?"

"No."

"But you'd like intelligent lighting, right?"

"No."

"An enhanced sound system?"

"No."

"Video footage from a drone?"

"No."

"Monogram projection?"

"No."

"So just one DJ?"

"He doesn't even have to be conscious. As long as he's cheap."

DJs do not come cheap, however. They don't even pretend to be. I had come directly to the bridal show from work and was still wearing my pleated pants and freshly ironed button-down Brooks Brothers shirt that I got for Christmas five years earlier. I'm sure they expected me to pull hundred dollar bills out of my ass like scarves from a magician's sleeve. Had I come dressed in my typical Levi's and an obscure graphic T-shirt, these vendors would've let me pass them by as they waited to pounce on a more monetarily meaty victim. But not even dressing like a penniless writer could keep the vacation agency vendors away. You'd need heavy-duty repellant—or even simple traps—to keep them at bay. They're as persistent as the seagulls down the shore, only louder.

After one of the DJs allowed us to escape, we were asked by a travel agent to fill out slips for a sweepstakes in which we could win a honeymoon to a destination of our choosing. Before this event, I hadn't even considered a honeymoon. I'd be shaking my piggy bank clean in order to make a dent in the impending wedding bills, so the last thing on my mind was where I could travel and sink further into debt. Maybe we could vacation at my grandparents' house in northern New Jersey, I thought about suggesting to Christine. It's all-inclusive. The residence is spotless; the meals are homemade; the TV shows are in Italian, and the arguments are authentic. If we don't leave the house, we would never know we weren't in Italy. Otherwise, our best chances of a proper honeymoon were through a sweepstakes.

A young woman who, during our brief conversation, kept reminding us that she had "no man" greeted us at the sweepstakes table, where we filled out the slips and handed them back to her. She held a perpetual smile, even as she spoke, and she regularly touched her face with her hands like she was kneading dough. In tune with every other vendor before her, she asked us if we had chosen a venue yet, where we were getting married, what our date was, and if we had put any thought into our honeymoon. When we told her that we had no clue what we were going to do after our wedding day, her eyes and smile grew like the unrestricted end of a stress ball.

"Well . . ." she began, grabbing a large binder and throwing it on the table in front of us. "Just because you're here with us today—*just* for you guys and no one else—I'm going to let you have a four-night, five-day stay at *any* of these places here." She opened the binder to the first page and pointed to a short list of destinations, including Grand Cayman, Bahamas, and Maui.

"*Or* you can get a *two*-night, *three*-day stay at any of these locations." She pointed to an even shorter list of destinations I didn't recognize.

"What's the catch?" Christine asked her, and the woman burst out laughing, sounding like the alarm of an old sedan.

"No catch, no catch!" she responded. "This is strictly marketing for us. You pay for the flight, and your stay is included. This is a way to show off our resorts to young guests, and hopefully you'll be coming back for years and years." The woman's smile didn't disappear, even despite our obvious skepticism, and I wondered at what point I should tell her we weren't interested. But she was such a buoyant saleswoman that I was fooled into believing that *maybe* this was legitimate.

The woman flipped through the binder to a photograph of an atrium inside a hotel. It was picturesque in the way that photos hanging on the walls of a dentist's office waiting room are picturesque. And, suddenly, my teeth began to hurt.

"All we need is for you to come take a tour of our hotel in New York City," she told us, pointing at the photo and nearly whispering that there'd also be a brief presentation. She closed the binder and pointed to the calendar pasted to its cover. "So what day works best for you? If you come during the weekend, we have meetings at nine in the morning, eleven in the morning, one in the afternoon, and two in the afternoon. I just need to see your I.D. and the credit card you'll be using for the refundable deposit."

"Wait, we have to pay?" I asked her.

"Yes, yes, I'm sorry! Just fifty dollars now, and you'll get that back as soon as you finish the tour of the hotel. We do it just in case you don't show up. It helps ensure that guests actually honor the appointment." She kept smiling and pointed back down to the cover of the binder. "So what day and time works best for you?"

I was figuring out a way to let her down easy and sneak away quickly when Christine asserted, "We're not interested."

The woman's smile drained from her face. Her eyes shrank a bit, and she scrunched her lips closed. She began to speak, but Christine said again, "Yeah, sorry, we're just not interested."

The woman slid the binder away from us, and nodded. "Good luck with everything," she said, more as a threat than a salutation.

Christine and I said good night to her and turned and walked into the precarious forest of wedding planners and entertainment companies. We'd be the prey underneath the suffocating paws of another salesperson, and I wondered if I could sprint straight out of the building without knocking anything over. That would be the only way I could possibly forgo speaking to anyone else. It wasn't like I could throw my hand up in someone's face and shout, "No! I don't want to talk to you!" The *whole reason* couples attended these events was to speak to the vendors, learn about their businesses, get an idea of price ranges, and book appointments with ones they liked. I'd be doing myself and my fiancée a disservice by walking around with my head down. But I felt like a lassoed hog in an old western. I was moments away from being tied by my haunches and hung over a campfire. Incidentally, *that* would've been a much better atmosphere than *this*.

This bridal show was nothing more than a four-dimensional telemarketing experience. Instead of sitting around at home waiting for solicitors to call, Christine and I went out of our way to visit them face to face. They were no more forgiving in person than they are on the phone. They were human mosquitoes. What made this experience even eerier was that it occurred during dinner time. That's the solicitors' witching hour.

It was another forty-five or so minutes of contact with unhelpful vendors before we made it back out into the hallway that divided the two rooms of the bridal show. We were about to re-enter the first room when I guided Christine down a separate hallway. We walked around the corner to another corridor that was empty, except for some janitors walking around. I put my back against the wall and sank to the floor, and Christine sat down next to me. Most of the vendors were happy to give us free stuff, but these free items consisted mainly of plastic bags and promotional flyers, which we stuffed into an even larger bag from Bed, Bath & Beyond.

As we sat on the carpeted floor of this seemingly safe hallway, we began rifling through the bag, pulling out the only items worth keeping: the snacks. That amounted to a couple chocolate chip cookies and candy bars.

By the end of the event, we were barely any closer to being prepared for our wedding, which was happening in less than a year. I tried not to vocalize our unpreparedness to Christine, partially because I didn't want to stress her out, but also because I was afraid more salespeople were slithering around this hallway like starved mole vipers, ready to pop out their heads and sink their teeth into the next couple who said, "We still have a lot of wedding planning to do."

I chomped on someone's pitiable attempt at a chocolate chip cookie and choked on what I believed were oats. I could hear that the rain outside was just dying down, and we'd be able to walk to our cars without getting soaked. I took that as a sign: *Get out as fast as you can.* But I stayed on the ground and continued eating.

Christine reached into her purse and pulled out a little book. I watched her flip through it as if she were fanning herself with the pages. It was her weekly planner with the Shakespeare quote on the front: *And though she be but little, she is fierce.*

Most people didn't study Shakespeare past junior or senior year of high school, yet he created words and sayings we still use today, just like this phrase that I've seen a number of women wear on their hoodies and handbags. In many cases, it doesn't accurately describe the women who own those products. In some cases, it does.

Christine slapped the planner shut. Then she looked at me and asked, "Should I cancel all of our appointments first thing tomorrow morning, or wait until the people contact me?" She didn't wait for me to respond. "Forget it. I don't care." She started to stand up, pinching the ends of her sundress as she rose. "Let's get the hell out of here."

ANOTHER TRAIN STORY

I nestled down next to a window for my ride back home from Newark Penn Station, placing my hulking backpack on the aisle seat next to me. I had ventured to New York Comic Con—as nerdy as it gets: alone—and I hid my purchases in every pocket of my bag. A *Breaking Bad-Dexter's Laboratory*-crossover T-shirt, a few vintage Flash comics, and some eclectic artwork, along with books I had brought with me to (unsuccessfully) get signed, all were squeezed inside. My casual black JanSport backpack was nowhere near as slim as it had been on the trip to the city. Now it looked like someone had inflated it with helium. I was afraid that the lightest bit of train turbulence would cause my backpack to explode like a piñata at a ten-year-old's birthday party. So I kept it close to my side and tried to look as unwilling as possible to move it. I clearly was not intim-idating in the slightest.

A woman dressed in the baby blue shirt and navy pants of a transit worker shuffled down the aisle. When she stopped at my seat, I noticed she wasn't wearing one of those porter's caps, nor was she carrying packs of stubs and slips in an apron wrapped around her waist. In fact, she looked rather unprepared to be collecting tickets from passengers. I didn't realize she was off-duty until she pointed at my backpack and asked, "Can I sit here?"

I counted to three before nodding and took my time moving my backpack to my lap. I wanted her to know how reluctant I was to give up the seat I had already chosen for my inanimate object. I couldn't understand why she needed to sit with the civilians, anyway. I suspected that NJ Transit had VIP seating for staff in some hidden section of the train. Or, more logically, if you're going to be on the train anyway, you might as well work until your stop—get paid that extra hour. She didn't *need* to sit here, and I think that's what frustrated me even more.

Without saying thank you, the woman threw her body onto the empty spot, and her large black duffle bag swung across her lap, nearly connecting with my backpack. Had I not stuck my knee up in time to block the collision, you would've read in the papers about a little Italian-American boy from New Jersey who made a pathetic backpack bomb out of rare comic books and overpriced art prints.

The woman took up all of her seat, and her pasty white arm wasn't afraid to get close to strangers who sat next to her on the train. Every few seconds, I'd get jabbed in the forearm by a stray elbow. I kept thinking she was nudging me to get my attention. But every time I looked up at her, she was staring at a different passenger. The train was nearly filled before she boarded, and she had her pick of a number of weirdo commuters to gawk at. I cozied up to the window and kept my bag bridged on my lap, both arms hugging it like a medicine ball.

Several minutes passed before the train finally left Newark Penn, and I kept counting down the stops in my head, anticipating her departing station. *Union. Please be Union. Or Roselle Park. Please get off by then. Maybe she'll get off at Cranford. Or Garwood!* The train made a point to stall at every station, but she never left.

By the time the train pulled into the Garwood station, her cell phone rang. She elbowed me a couple more times as she unzipped a pocket in her duffle bag. She reached inside and pulled out a gray flip phone. After she looked at the caller ID, she sighed, flipped the phone open, put it to her ear, and barked, "Hello? Hello? Eric? Eric? Hello? Eric?" The woman barely offered a pause in between words, giving the other party no time to answer. After a few seconds, she took the phone away from her ear, closed it, and stuck it back in her bag.

The train rattled as it rolled down the tracks, approaching the Westfield station. After nearly five stops, I noticed that the conductor still had not come to take my ticket, which was for the best, because I just then realized that I couldn't find it. As I was searching my wallet for the little pink stub, the woman's phone rang again. She flipped it open and put it to her ear.

"Hello?" she said into her phone, whispering this time. I assumed her caller actually decided to respond, because the next thing the woman said was, "Hi, Eric . . . Yeah, I know it's ya birthday, so I just wanted to send ya ma blessings . . . Ya welcome . . . Did ya hear about David?" A few seconds passed. She removed the phone from her ear again and gazed at its tiny screen before putting it back up against her face. "I said, *Did ya hear about David*?" she yelled. "He lost a toe . . . I said he lost a toe . . . Yeah, from the diabeetus." She snapped her tongue on the roof of her mouth in disappointment several times before continuing. "When's your operation?" she asked. "I said, when's your operation?"

The train stopped in Fanwood, and she jolted forward but didn't stand up to leave.

"Damn train," she whispered. "I'll see ya at your operation then, Eric . . . Obviously I'm not going to be there *during* your operation. I'll see ya afterward."

A train conductor finally made his way into our car as the train started again. The woman reached into her bag and pulled out a small, wallet-looking item. I continued to dig through the pockets of my backpack, and sweat began to fizzle on the crest of my forehead as the conductor got closer and closer to my row. When he was standing next to our seats, the woman, phone still pressed against her ear, flipped open her wallet in the same way she did her phone moments before. She raised the wallet and presented whatever was inside to the conductor. He nodded, pulled a thin white sheet from the pocket of his apron, punctured it a couple times with his hole puncher, and stuck it in the headrest of the seat in front of us. That indicated that she was free to be a passenger on this train, free from any harassment of an impatient conductor.

"And, sir?" he questioned, switching his attention to me.

"Ummm . . ." I continued scouring my belongings for the peskiest ticket I've purchased yet. I couldn't find it anywhere—not in my jeans pockets, backpack pockets, or inside either of my shoes. I thought about checking in between the pages of the books I had with me, but I knew myself. If I opened just one cover, I would've gotten distracted and started reading.

I knew I had purchased a ticket for the ride home, but I didn't know what I had done with it. I feared I accidentally might have used it to pay for a hot dog. I could've bought twenty of them for the price of a single one-way NJ Transit ticket. Or maybe I used it to dispose of my gum before I had that dirty-water dog for lunch. Whatever I did with it, I knew I wasn't finding it during this trip.

"Sir, your ticket," the conductor pressed.

I decided I was going to give up, pay the two hundred eighty-five dollars—or whatever it was—to purchase a rail ticket while on board. But I had no cash with me. There was no way I was going to trade one of my comics for a ticket. He could kick me off the train if he wanted. I was in no hurry to get home. Besides, I had plenty of reading material to keep me occupied for at least a week, if it came down to it.

I thought maybe I could make a break for it, hop over these seats and into another railcar before any transit employees had time to react. But I couldn't do it with this elephantine corpse of a backpack I was carrying around with me. I didn't know what other option I had. I needed to just tell him I didn't have a ticket and face the very miniscule, trivial consequences I was so afraid of for some reason.

When the conductor looked like he was going to ask me for my ticket a third time, the woman sitting next to me, the one who commandeered my backpack's seat a half hour earlier, put her hand up to the conductor. "He's good," she said, phone still to her ear.

I froze in a compromising position, one arm reaching into my back pocket, the other deep inside my backpack. I looked at the woman, and she smiled at me. The conductor nodded and walked away.

Just moments before, I had contemplated wrapping the arm loop of my backpack around her head until all Eric could hear were muffled screams. Now, I wanted to hug this woman, or perhaps just give her a limp handshake.

These preconceived notions that had been festering in my mind seemed to dissolve like the train ticket I had once kept in my pocket. Had she really elbowed me several times in the forearm, or was I just sitting too close to her? Did she really speak so loudly into her cell phone? Does that even matter? After all, it's not like we're in the quiet car anyway. She seemingly transformed from Carrot Top to Bono with just one generous act, and I turned into the fool, a fool who felt the smooth, flimsy paper of an NJ Transit ticket stub between his fingers as he swiped the inside-bottom of his backpack.

There it was: underneath my comics and novelty apparel,

where I had slipped it hours earlier for safe keeping. I resolved to let that ticket rest there. If I pulled it out of my bag, she possibly wouldn't have noticed. Or, more likely, I would've become her next topic of interest in her conversation with Eric.

"Ah, man, Eric, you'll never believe what this little hairy boy just pulled over on me," she might've said.

I slipped my arm out of my backpack, ticketless, and I took my other hand out of my back pocket. "Thank you," I told her, smiling what I imagined was a narrow, crooked smile.

The woman bobbed her head and turned to gaze straight ahead, the phone fastened to her cheek.

"Is Anthony coming?" she shouted into the phone. "I want to know if Anthony's coming." After a few seconds passed: "To the operation, dummy!"

RENT OR FLOWERS?

The starting cost for wedding flowers in the United States is fifteen hundred dollars. Let that sink in, as I did, sulking in my chair at my soon-to-be mother-in-law's dining room table. It was about eight months before Christine's and my wedding day, just weeks before the COVID-19 pandemic shut down the entire country. I was struggling to fit the remainder of my mac and cheese onto my fork when Christine stated that she wanted simple bouquets for the wedding.

"Just something for me and my maid of honor and each of my bridesmaids to carry," she related. "Nothing crazy."

Well, "nothing crazy" amounted to *one thousand five hundred dollars*. By that assessment, edible gold on a hot fudge sundae or a parka made from lynx fur is nothing crazy. That kind of money could get us a six-tier chocolate fountain and keep it replenished for *years*. That's tuition for a semester at a community college or a fourteen-year subscription to Netflix.

Fifteen hundred dollars could get me a brand new laptop so I could ditch the relic that's crashed nine times in the couple hours it's taking me to write this essay. The *stupidest* thing I could think to do with fifteen hundred dollars was put it toward our student-loan debt, and that's *still* better than spending it on some shrubs.

When I voiced these opinions, I was told not to speak of flowers, flower petals, bouquets, wreaths, center pieces, or potted plants ever again, even years after the ceremony and reception had passed. At one point or another during wedding planning, I had complained about each of those items and their costs, so Christine and her mother decided I would play no role in deciding which flowers, or how many, would be chosen for the ceremony and reception. Yet, I was forced to listen to their discussions of flowers while prohibited from uttering a word, my first foray into marriage preparation.

My mother-in-law agreed that Christine would need a bouquet for herself and slightly smaller ones for her maid of honor and bridesmaids. She added that we'd need boutonnieres for about a dozen men as well as corsages for the mothers and grandmothers. Then we also could use a few arrangements for the church and maybe a couple for the reception venue.

Christine's mom offered to pay for the flowers. Well, she didn't exactly offer; she told us she'd be paying for them. She didn't give us a choice, though we hardly put up a fight, I'll admit. I was thankful I didn't have to worry about that cost too, but I care about her finances just as much as I do my own. Or maybe it's the principle of the thing. Wedding flowers just *shouldn't* cost that much money.

American weddings seem to use an overabundance of flowers, as if these floras themselves are officiating the matrimony. Each individual item is priced twenty-times more than its worth, by my calculations. I imagined that each wedding requires a half-acre garden—just a field overgrown with thousands of peonies, lilies, roses, tulips, and every other obscure genome of flower. The fields would sit among the fumaroles of an active volcano off the coast of Hawaii, and they would be accessible exclusively by seaplane. The flowers could only be picked twice a year and must be preserved in a special liquid concoction composed of volcanic ash and ocean water. The labor of growing and collecting these flowers would be excruciating, and florists could therefore justify charging thousands of dollars for various bouquets and arrangements.

In reality, though, the process is far less strenuous.

Flowers do not dictate the quality of a wedding. Beyond the venue, food, and music, people hardly notice the decorations you've spent long, grueling months slaving to complete. Midway through the reception, guests will forget that someone even got married. They're typically more focused on the bar and the dance floor. If someone *does* happen to comment on any of the floral arrangements, that means they've spent too much time at the bar, and by the morning they'll have forgotten all about your choice in florist.

That choice just isn't so crucial that engaged couples should be dropping rent payments for floral arrangements. Realistically, flowers should cost less than tickets to a Yankees game.

As it turned out, it would've been cheaper to buy our guests grandstand tickets for Yankee Stadium than to decorate a wedding venue with flowers.

Peonies, lilies, roses, and tulips are all sold at grocery shops year round, and they remain steady at a reasonable cost, except near Valentine's Day and Mother's Day. But should you tell a florist that you're getting married, they'll immediately quadruple the price of a twenty-nine-dollar bouquet, then tell you that's a discount.

I suggested that Christine tell the florist these flowers were for a funeral rather than a wedding. People go easy on you when they think someone you love has died.

"Yes," we could've told them, "our Uncle Remus passed away, so can we just get eleven tasteful boutonnieres and four corsages for his funeral, please?"

Come to think of it, if we told the florist that this was going to be a double funeral, she might've felt so badly for us that she would've donated six bouquets for free. If Christine and I worked in some fake tears and a loud, awkward sob or two, the florist might've even thrown in some beautiful wreaths. Pity wreaths are the highlight of any fashionable wedding.

Christine didn't go for any of these golden suggestions, though, and instead prohibited me from engaging in any discussion pertaining to flowers. However, no one's forbidden me from writing about them.

THE GIFT

What's the appropriate way to act when you stumble upon a pile of human waste?

I don't think I'll ever get used to it, no matter how many cities I visit. It's everywhere these days. On dressing room floors, between the cushions of movie theater seats, in cardboard boxes under subway benches. It's often inconspicuous and shy, only given away by the rank fetor. Most men will pass right by these dense logs and get lunch that same afternoon without another thought. It's only *really* surprising when you find poop at work. Then it's too personal. Our jobs are already riddled with misfortunes. A jammed copier here, a faulty fire alarm there. But turd-bedazzled rugs shouldn't be one of them.

Finding poop in an office space is like discovering a trout hanging on a tree branch. Your first thought hones in on the stench before you wonder, "*Who's responsible for this?*"

Rogue poop in the workplace is a "gift," more or less. Sure, it's not wrapped or donning some baroque bow, but whoever delivered it has no intention of taking it back, as if to say, "I put a lot of thought and effort into this one." It's not an expensive present, but it's homemade, and parents teach their kids it's the thought that counts.

During the height of the pandemic, I was charged with revising a unit training manual. It was mostly busy work, but I still dedicated too much time to it, to the point where I blocked out everything else around me. Several days before my wedding, I holed myself up in my office for the better part of an afternoon working on this manual. When I finished rewriting specific sections, I sent them to a printer down the hall, to the right of the men's restroom, which was just outside my office

On many occasions, I stepped into the hallway to inhale the rancid odor of whatever foul substances vacated the bowels of my seventy-year-old colleague, Larrid. Back when my office door would be open throughout the work day, I used to occasionally hear him rattle the knob of the bathroom door before bursting out, hiking up his pants with his unwashed hands as he did so. The fog of sulfur would waft behind and follow him through the corridor, a toxic cape tied to his back. Being immediately across from the restroom, I had exclusive access to his wretched manmade odor that violated my olfactory epithelium. I'd have to spend an entire month consuming nothing but Wendy's and Rockstar energy drinks in order to produce these caliber stenches, but Larrid could do it with just a Wawa coffee and an egg sandwich for breakfast. It was a hostile work environment, but I had trouble submitting a complaint that read, *Larrid's shit stinks*. It would've given a whole new meaning to the term "entitlement."

On this afternoon, I swung open my office door, hoping to make a quick round trip to the printer without being spotted. Immediately, I was rushed by a gust of dank wind, the kind you'd expect in your backyard if it bordered a landfill. Even with a surgical mask covering half my face, I could smell *and* taste it. I realized then that this was why the chief medical advisor to the President suggested everyone wear *two* masks. The potency was both disturbing and impressive, in the way that MMA injuries typically are. The men's room door was wide open, and it smelled like the log was still floating in the latrine like a decomposing life raft.

I bolted down the hallway to where the printer sat, retrieved my pages, and retreated back to my cave. After I slammed my door closed, I figured that this was as much time as I should spend thinking about another man's bowel movements during a workday. In fact, it was nearing the end of my shift, so I packed my laptop bag and exited my office, holding my breath this time as I opened the door. I turned left out of my office and toward the building's exit. I kept my head low, as one would do when walking through a burning building. Stenches rise, like heat and smoke, so this was the safest course of action.

No more than two paces past the men's bathroom door, I saw the gift. It sat right in the middle of the hallway carpet: a dollop of milky turd. A mini biscuit drenched in homemade gravy. A slug covered in wet sand.

The ophidian odor slithered through the fibers of my mask again, and I gagged behind this useless PPE. It was a natural stink bomb, the kind teenagers would steal from thrift shops. But this one was much worse than the ones I remembered as a kid.

When I was around twelve years old, my mother bought my brothers and me bags of what she thought were candy. They were about the size of a sack of Cracker Jacks. The design on the outside depicted animated soldiers and mushroom clouds of nuclear explosions. The writing on the packaging was mostly cryptic warning labels, and there were no nutrition facts printed anywhere. None of us could figure out what kind of candy was inside, but since my mom got these from a novelty shop in northern New Jersey, we all were intrigued.

I tried opening mine like a bag of potato chips, but the plastic was thick and the adhesive used to bind the sides was too strong. When I realized I couldn't rip the bag open, I instead squeezed its bottom with one hand to try to pop it open. I was sitting on my grandmother's couch, and not wanting to get mysterious candy all over the brown leather and macramé blankets, I covered the top of the bag with my other hand. I squeezed as hard as I could with my bottom hand, until I heard something pop inside it. The packaging, though, didn't rip. It was like one of those ice packs with the interior bag that has to break before you press it against a black eye. I stopped squeezing and held the bag in my palm and watched as it expanded like a water balloon under a running faucet. It continued to expand, even when I tried to pack it down like a snowball. My mother and brothers stood around me, watching the bag in my hand grow larger and larger. When it inflated to the size and shape of a softball, it froze for a few seconds. Everyone else stepped back. I didn't move from the couch. I thought it was finished, but in my hand, I could feel a substance sizzling inside. *These might be Pop Rocks*, I thought, still somehow convinced this was candy.

The bag split open and exploded in an instant. A greenish-brown pudding-like substance splattered all over my legs and new cargo shorts. After about five seconds, I began to smell it—a combination of deviled eggs and deer carcasses. It was as if I had been vomited on by a kindergartener.

It was a stink bomb. A gag gift you get for someone you socialize with but secretly dislike. It was devastating, because it had been a gift from my mother—*and* she had gotten more for her two other sons. Even after a shower and change of clothes, the scent still lingered, as if I had been sprayed by a skunk.

To this day, my mom claims she knew what it was. "Obviously I wouldn't mistake a stink bomb for candy, Patrick," she tells me. But she doesn't realize that sounds worse than the alternative.

The gift Larrid left for me several days before I was to be married was astronomically more aggressive in stench than that manufactured stink bomb, which was produced from a variety of non- and semi-toxic chemicals. The stink bomb was made at least fifteen years prior, when toxicity and deadliness were more of a goal than a concern, yet Larrid was still able to outdo this company with just his natural waste.

After I saw it, I stormed down the hall to alert a coworker. If someone held their head high and stomped through the office hallway, unaware of this fecal landmine, their stepping in it would only cause more problems. *And* if I knew about it and didn't warn anyone, that could turn out worse for me than the stench alone.

As I traveled farther from ground zero, I started to come to my senses. I imagined Larrid, humiliated and disoriented, racing out to his car to find a change of clothes, his boar-like figure rambling down the stairs in discomfort. I had been furious with Larrid for defecating on the floor of our office, but it never occurred to me that he may have done this by accident, soiled his pants before he could make it to the restroom. It was unreasonable to assume that he intentionally was trailing his feces behind him like a sickly Hansel and Gretel.

I don't know if it was the maddening scent that was scrambling my brainwaves or if the initial anger relinquished any humanity inside me and simply created a veil of hatred. That's what is tough about going straight to anger when something unfortunate happens—my brain seems to hold its breath, trapping any and all rationality and understanding inside like a hostage. It enables the Mr. Hyde traits to sneak out, and I'm left making choices that only sink me deeper into unfounded anger and hatred.

When I let my brain breathe again, I wasn't as angry with Larrid as I had been just moments before. He didn't drop that noxious slug outside my office on purpose. This was likely an accident. Or, if this definitely wasn't an accident, it was Larrid's form of presenting a gift, an early wedding present, I supposed. I wouldn't take it home with me, however.

I planned to tell Christine that my coworker had baked us some brownies, but he dropped them in the hallway on his way to deliver them. She'd be touched by the gesture but devastated by the outcome. In a way, that's how I felt then, too.

IT'S YOUR DAY

No one has written a rulebook for planning a wedding during a pandemic. Sure, there are guidelines for organizing a wedding during a non-pandemic year. These mostly are found in books with expensive floral arrangements depicted on the covers. They're typically directed at the brides-to-be and make remarks like, "Pick the flowers you love for your wedding. It's *your* day," "Select your favorite music to play during the reception. It's *your* day," and "Hire at least six photographers—unless your father is paying, then at least eight. It's *your* day." Each guideline has a positive, reassuring message for the bride, telling her to breathe, take time to stop and enjoy the planning, and make sure to deplete her funds in the process. If you don't go bankrupt planning your wedding, why get married in the first place?

While organizing our wedding, Christine and I (mostly Christine) consulted several different marriage preparation books and websites. They all said pretty much the same thing, as if they were written by students copying each other's English homework. One might read, "It's *your* day," while the other would proclaim, "The day is *yours*." As nauseatingly repetitive as it was to read those statements, the sentiment is important to remember, because the point is simple: This event is for you and your loved one, so screw what everyone else thinks. This is true during a normal wedding, and it's even more crucial to keep in mind during a pandemic wedding.

The majority of people who had their weddings during this COVID-19 public health crisis were planning during normal times. One day, our political leaders decided to close everything down—restaurants, gyms, tattoo parlors, and every other type of venue. They told us to wear masks and stay away from people. They gave us a little money to keep us calm and basically wished us "good luck" while they retreated to their mansions. Medical personnel scrambled; first responders scrambled; independent business owners, teachers, entrepreneurs, and even major corporations were left in the dust. To a much lesser extent, those couples who dipped into their savings accounts with snow shovels to fund their weddings felt as though someone had taken a bite out of their hindquarters.

Christine and I were due to wed during the summer of 2020, giving us more than four months of distance between the beginning of the pandemic in the United States and our big day. However, we had only about two months to decide what we were going to do: Would we postpone until next year or move forward with a restricted pandemic wedding?

Naturally, we consulted our guidebooks. All had chapters on venues, food, music, flowers, photographers, videographers, and guest lists, but none advised what to do in the event that a dangerous respiratory-attacking virus is being spread throughout the entire world. The books all immediately became useless.

When the pandemic hit, we, like every other engaged couple on the planet, had to make a decision. During these emotional couple months, we received a lot of advice—coincidentally from people who never had to make a pressing decision during a pandemic. In fact, a lot of the people who told us what to do didn't even have to plan or fund their own weddings, let alone while the world was burning to the ground.

"Just push everything out until next year," my mom suggested. "What's the rush?"

Christine and I had been together for eight years by this point. We got engaged after seven years of dating. There obviously was no rush. But when you spend an entire year excited to marry your favorite person in the world, it's not so easy to wait even longer. On top of that, tomorrow (or *next year*, for that matter) isn't promised. People were losing loved ones; they were separated from family and friends; jobs and homes were lost. Even though we were fortunate during this time, we didn't know if everyone would be there to celebrate in 2021, especially with a virus being spread faster than legs in a brothel. Christine and I gave our books another look, and they reminded us whose day it really was: *ours*.

If I ever were to write one of these wedding-planning books, I know what the number-one rule would be: don't let anyone make you forget that your wedding is about you and your partner. People will unkindly suggest that "the ceremony is for the couple, but the reception is for the guests."

Fuck that.

The ceremony is for the couple, *and* the reception is for the couple, as well as the hours before the ceremony and the after-party following the reception. If there were more than twenty-four hours in a day, *those* would be for the couple, too.

Of course you want your guests to enjoy themselves, but that doesn't mean it's about them. It's not just okay to be selfish on your wedding day—it's *required*. (Just please don't turn into a tyrant on my account; the whole idea is for you to enjoy yourself, and you can't do that if you're scrutinizing everything about the day. In these instances, a little apathy goes a long way.)

Marriage is about love. A wedding is the formal union of two people on the foundation of their unyielding love for each other. It's built upon the premise (and the cliché) that you would do anything for your partner and their health and happiness. Just to make them happy, you'd do something painful and gut-wrenching, like plan a wedding.

The ceremony is sacred, and its key components are the couple—not the congregation, not the floral arrangements, not the music, not the venue. The reception that follows is the celebration of that union, of that love. We eat because we love to eat; we dance because we love to dance; we talk and laugh and sing and cry because we love to talk and laugh and sing and cry. Your friends and your family members, who help to fill out the pews in your church or the seats at your ceremony, help us to celebrate, because *they* love us, too. (See how it comes full circle?) They witness the proclamations of faith, adoration, and unity, and they witness two people's vows of lifelong commitment to each other, and they partake in the festivities. In the grand scheme of matrimony though, their presence is momentary. Yes, it's cherished, but it's still momentary. After you remove your tux or dress or overalls, the only element of that occasion that continues day after day is the unrelenting love one partner has for the other. It can't be complicated by what other people think your wedding should be like.

Yeah, I know that more than half of all marriages end in divorce, and some of the ones that don't, end in murder-suicide. But not many people marry with the intent to get divorced, and I hope no one marries with the thought of killing their spouse. It would completely unravel my argument. Also, it's bad.

Christine and I decided to have a pandemic wedding ceremony, keeping it as small as possible in order to prevent the spread of the virus. We pushed our reception out a full year, hoping that by then we could fill the venue with our loved ones. We weren't the first couple in history to marry during a pandemic, and we won't be the last. Pandemics are inevitable. They aren't limited to just viral outbreaks, either. There are continuous outbreaks of stupidity and misinformation. In that regard, every couple gets married during a pandemic, whether they realize it or not.

When we told our family members our plan, no one was enthused.

"You're not going to want to have a reception next year," Christine's dad told her. He eventually added, "I'm just letting you know—because I don't want you to get upset—some people might not come to your reception, because you're already married. It's just weird."

"No shit it's weird," Christine retorted. "This whole year has been weird. People all over the world had to make *weird* decisions, because this hasn't happened in the past century." After a breath, she added, "That's fine if someone doesn't want to come. I'm not forcing anyone to do anything. We want to celebrate with the people who actually want to be there."

Christine's father was right. Some invited guests didn't want to come to the reception a year later. Many of them didn't even let us know, because RSVP-ing during a pandemic evidently is too difficult.

I agree that having a reception a year after a ceremony is weird. But as Christine conveyed to her father, if you got through 2020 and 2021 without being at least a little strange, you likely were completely oblivious to the virus that was ravaging countries around the world, infecting and killing countless individuals. People were *disinfecting their produce*! So I'd argue that Christine and I were on the lower end of the spectrum of weirdness, along with mask wearing and social distancing.

We made our decisions, "weird" or otherwise. As I said, no one provided us with a rulebook for how to plan a wedding during a pandemic. If they had, and if it said anything that contradicted "Do what makes you happy," I would've thrown it right into the trash—or tried to sell it on eBay. I wouldn't judge you if you were to do the same. Actually, I'd encourage you to do so, and to do what makes you happy. After all, it's *your* day, and the day is *yours*.

THE PROBLEM IS . . .

'm elbow-deep in a cardboard box filled with books from my childhood, and I find a bookmark folded from a loose-leaf sheet of paper. It's wedged between *Lou Gehrig: The Luckiest Man* and *Where the Sidewalk Ends*. I must've been seven when I folded it, a time when picture books were a struggle to finish in one sitting. I never dared dog-ear a single page, so I'd make bookmarks out of the nearest materials. Baseball cards, mechanical pencils, mini calculators, colorful pipe cleaners, and sheets of paper all became my bookmarks at one time or another. This one, now of drinking age, still clings to the stories of my youth.

I don't throw away the bookmark. I tuck it into *Lou Gehrig: The Luckiest Man,* at the climax of the story, when Gehrig swings his bat and the ball goes nowhere, when he falls down while getting dressed, when he exercises more but only gets frailer.

I had read this book so many times in elementary school that I was able to recite it word for word without cracking open the cover. It's based on a true story: the life, career, and untimely demise of one of the greatest athletes of all time.

I flip through it a few times before putting it down. I had wanted to save all my old picture books for my future kids. Will these sit on a little white-washed bookcase one day or stay untouched in a cardboard box for another twenty-one years?

The first time my wife was pregnant was fall 2021. I spent the majority of the time *outside* the waiting room at her OB/GYN's office, on pleather seats next to the elevators. Because of adjusted protocols during the COVID-19 pandemic, only patients could wait inside the actual waiting room.

We were five stories high, on the top floor of a hospital. I stared out the window at the tiny people walking from car to building, building to car. During our initial visit, I watched for an hour before Christine poked her head out the door behind me. "They're ready for us."

She guided me through another door and then a third, into a dark room housing a computer and a medical bed with stirrups attached at the end. A small blond woman with a soft voice followed us in. When she began Christine's first ultrasound, she tilted the screen so we could see it. But I had no idea what I was looking at. I thought I saw a deflated ping pong ball in a dusting of cigarette ash. That couldn't be the inside of my wife's uterus, could it? I imagined doctors and sonographers mocking us as we walked out of their office that day. "Can you believe it?" one of the docs would exclaim to the tech. "*Another* patient fell for the fake-ultrasound gag! How could they not tell it's a close-up of a George Foreman Grill?!" Then they'd laugh and wipe tears of joy from their eyes with hundred-dollar bills.

For the time being, though, our tech was somber. She didn't talk to us, just clicked away on her keyboard several dozen times. After a few moments, she pointed to the ping pong ball on the screen. "See that there?" Her index finger closed in on the white oval inside a larger black circle surrounded by gray static. "That's the yolk sac."

"Uh oh," Christine said, but I didn't know why.

"No, no 'uh oh' yet," the tech responded. "It's a little small for how far along you said you are, but we'll have the doctor review the results and discuss with you both immediately."

Then we were back out of the office, Christine in the waiting room and I in the hallway. After another half hour passed, the doctor—a male for some reason—called us into his office.

"The problem is . . ." he began. This was how he started most of his sentences—with the car-mechanic method of identifying an issue.

You shouldn't start *any* conversation with "The problem is," especially if you're a physician. If you start a sentence with "The problem is . . ." I'll have to argue that the *real* problem is we need a better doctor. Preferably female.

But that's how he started the conversation anyway. Then he paused for several hours. Or maybe seconds. He said, "It may just be too early to tell anything. The yolk sac is too small. We can't see a heartbeat. The problem is . . . there may be one of two things wrong, but we don't know yet."

The first possibility, he explained, was that we had made an error when calculating our dates. "Most couples, especially when they first start trying, don't pay as close attention to the calendar as they think. Right now, it looks like you're only five or six weeks along." The other possibility was that something may be wrong with the way the embryo was developing. "The problem is, we just don't know right now. We'll have you come back in two weeks to do another ultrasound to see if the yolk sac has grown at all."

Christine and I spent the next two weeks maintaining our regular schedules. Working, working, working, and working. And then when we had some free time, we worked some more. With four jobs between the two of us, we didn't have a moment to stop and feel sorry for ourselves. Although Christine suspected that something was wrong, we just didn't know. We were pushed out of the doctor's office with virtually no concrete answers, and the excitement of having a child was beginning to fizzle. It was feeling more like a fantasy than a reality.

The problem was, we *might* have had a problem. But other people, perhaps even patients in the office that day, *did* actually have problems that needed to be dealt with.

After we walked out of the doctor's office that day, Christine went down the hall for a brief examination and to get bloodwork done, and I went back outside to wait, this time ignoring the windows beside me. While I tried to make myself comfortable in a pleather chair, another couple exited the office. They stood in front of the elevator, the uncomfortable silence interrupted only by the mechanical dinging as the car passed every floor on the way up.

"What do we have to do again?" the man eventually whispered.

The woman looked down at the dull yellow and cream-colored papers she held in her hands. "This … I have to get blood-work," she said slowly, hushed.

"Again?" the man asked.

"It's *okay*."

The elevator doors opened, and they both sauntered in and dropped five floors below.

We returned to the office exactly two weeks later, but not before Christine requested a different doctor—the only female physician employed by that office.

I didn't—and still don't—understand why men are allowed to be in this specific field. Sure, these other male doctors have years of education and experience and are probably qualified at this point, but not only are women naturally smarter and more caring and adept than men, they also *have* the genitalia that they're examining. Men should stick with being general physicians, surgeons, and penis doctors. All I'm saying is: stop touching my wife's privates!

Fortunately, the same *female* sonographer from the first visit conducted Christine's second ultrasound. This time, on that screen, we saw nothing. No yolk sac, no flickering heartbeat. Just a dirty ashtray.

Christine stared at the monitor and then her head snapped toward me. Her face red, pupils dilated, all she managed was a mousy "Pat" before twisting her head back to the screen.

Twenty minutes later, we were called into the office of the female OB/GYN. This new doctor had wiry yellow hair and pale skin. Her voice was as soft as the ultrasound tech's but a few octaves higher. Christine and I made ourselves comfortable in her guest chairs, and she strolled in after us.

"I don't have good news for *you*," she said, in a sing-songy way, as if she were talking to her Yorkie after running out of puppy chow. I prayed she was in the wrong room, but she sat down behind the desk and continued. "The yolk sac collapsed. The pregnancy failed. I'm sorry."

Christine was no longer pregnant. The doctor told us it wasn't because of anything we did. Nothing Christine ate, not a vigorous workout or long walk made this happen. "It's just bad luck," the doctor said. That was her medical diagnosis. Bad luck. As if we had just lost four hundred dollars in a slot machine or got a shoe lace stuck in between escalator steps. The problem is, we have a clinical case of misfortune, apparently.

Christine went back a week later to get bloodwork done. They conducted another ultrasound to see if her miscarriage was progressing. "My insurance doesn't cover these ultrasounds,"

Christine said. "Are they buy one, get one free?"

The technician performing the ultrasound, the same woman as the last two times, told Christine of her own miscarriage. She was five months along when she lost the baby. "I went on to have four healthy boys," she added.

Four women Christine had worked with at the time had five miscarriages among them, all during different stages of their respective pregnancies. I found out that a close relative of mine had three, all during the third trimesters. The only bright side to any of this is that all five women eventually went on to have healthy pregnancies, just like the ultrasound tech. A miscarriage isn't indicative of future pregnancies. It only speaks to this one.

The doctor prescribed Christine two doses of a medication that could progress the miscarriage. It would help the uterus push the collapsed sac out of her body. She told Christine to take the first dose later that week, if she wanted. But in the middle of the week, Christine left work early. It was beginning to happen. I met her at home that afternoon.

Early in the evening, Christine's cramping became severe. She couldn't stand up, but then she couldn't sit or lie down either. She slowly crawled up the stairs and into the bathroom. Nothing was comforting. She tried to take a bath but ended up taking a scalding hot shower until the water turned cold. She screamed and at times fought back tears. Her hair had been tied into a tight bun and gradually unfolded around her shoulders as the night progressed.

Despite the intense pain, she never looked lesser. Her hazel eyes bore into me whenever she caught me staring. When I slipped my fingers between hers, she'd squeeze, and every ounce of strength was still there, knuckles white for minutes before she'd release. I tried to make myself useful—arranged the bed with a heating pad, got her water and snacks. I listened to her, spoke to her, let her know that this wasn't forever. The uterus was trying to help get rid of what was inside her, and then when it was gone, the cramping would stop. She said it helped, but she was just humoring me. I couldn't actually help. I was Neosporin for a gunshot wound.

A couple hours passed before the cramping slowed, then stopped completely late at night. By the next day, Christine was dressed and ready to go back to the doctor's office for another examination. Of the two hours we were at the office, ninety-five minutes were spent waiting. This time, Christine sat outside the waiting area with me.

A different tech conducted the ultrasound, which showed that the sac was out of Christine's uterus. When the doctor later conducted a deeper examination, she found the sac in her cervix. Christine was on another medical bed, lying on her back, legs raised in metal stirrups. The doctor pulled out the sac with cold metal tongs, identical to ones you'd use when grilling hotdogs.

When the wiry-haired doctor said, "All done," Christine didn't reply. She rolled her body to the side, facing the wall. The doctor stepped over to her and gave her a conserved hug. "You've been *so* strong throughout all this. *So* strong. You're the only one I've ever seen get this far without crying. I kept wondering when we were going to see those tears . . . Let it out. It's okay. You *will* go on to have a healthy pregnancy."

Then, the doctor stood up straight and walked out of the room. We never saw her again.

However, we did see all the bills. Repeatedly. In case you're wondering how much it costs to have a miscarriage during the first trimester, it's about as costly as a tiger cub on the black market. Every visit, every ultrasound, every seat we sat on inside and outside the waiting room—they all cost an inordinate amount of money. As Christine had mentioned, her health insurance would cover virtually nothing. They let her review her claims on a fancy smartphone app, but we couldn't figure out what any of it meant.

Medical insurance claims are intentionally written in an extraterrestrial gibberish that only about point-zero-zero-zero-zero-two percent of the world's population can decipher. I wouldn't be surprised if employees of medical insurance companies were in the process of learning to write in ancient Egyptian hieroglyphs so that *no one* would ever understand how to read them again. At first glance, a trip to the doctor appears to cost as much as the U.S. deficit, plus your firstborn child. In reality, it costs only one trillion dollars and half your lunch every day for the next six years.

Healthcare is designed to be unaffordable. That gives it the illusion of prestige that's associated with institutions like Princeton University and luxury box seats at NFL stadiums. It doesn't matter that ninety-four percent of your time at doctors' offices is spent waiting for the doctor to call you into her office and talk to you for a total of eighty-six seconds. It's still going to be a three-hundred-dollar visit. And everyone experiences the stress of medical bills at one time or another. We're not refined androids who require minimal maintenance. We've got bodies that save and attack us on a daily basis.

About a week after my mom found out about the miscarriage, she told Christine that a relative also was having some health issues. Possibly polycystic ovary syndrome. It's a hormonal disorder that can cause even further health concerns, like diabetes, high blood pressure, and uterine cancer.

"I think your mom was trying to make me feel better, letting me know that I'm not the only one going through something, but that only made me feel worse," Christine told me. "It doesn't help knowing loved ones are suffering, too."

After a few moments sitting silently at the kitchen table, Christine joked, "What am I supposed to do? Call her to see who's suffering more?"

If Christine had been serious, no one would have minded. My entire family loves competition. "What about me?" is shouted more at our holiday dinners than "Pass the parmesan." Everyone tries to outdo each other with their stories about working, cooking, driving, shopping, and vacationing. Illness is no different.

"Do you have severe cramping?"

"Nonstop."

"You bleeding?"

"Excessively."

"From your womanly parts?"

"Yup, and sometimes my nose."

"Did something die inside you?"

"No."

"Whelp, looks like I win."

Christine and I often forget that trauma isn't a competition. Just because someone lost their baby at a later stage—or even after birth—doesn't mean that we have no right to grieve. You can't just shake yourself out of a funk or learn and grow by reminding yourself that countless other people have more of a right to be sad than you do. Telling ourselves that we're not going to dwell on something because someone else is suffering worse is *not* dealing with a problem.

Even people who experience the same shock grieve differently. Christine grieved differently from me, because she was the one carrying. She had to be the specimen under the microscope all those times at the doctor's office. She was the one who spent hours writhing in pain at the base of a scalding hot shower while her body expelled what was supposed to become her first child. She was the one who bled and bled and was fogged by the agony and resonating aches that stayed with her body for the following few weeks. I just watched. I was a dog chained to a fence just barking at the problem, hoping I was making it better somehow. I was present and at her whim and held her, but I didn't experience the torment that Christine did. The miscarriage affected every part of her, physically, mentally, emo-tionally. She even stepped differently for a little while afterward, because her feet just couldn't land the same way.

The aftermath was like one of those videos of a shoreline following a hurricane. It was quiet in the house, a little messy with towels tossed haphazardly at the hamper, bedsheets twisted into pretzels, the trash can filled with pad wrappers and tissues. While Christine felt better the next morning, I knew neither of us really would feel much better for a little while.

Christine's yolk sac never exceeded the size of a blueberry. It wasn't nearly a baby, technically, but to a soon-to-be parent, it's a baby as soon as there's a plus sign on the pregnancy test. You make plans and worry about upcoming weddings and events you may not be able to attend in eight months. You picture your guest room as a nursery and think about what fur-niture is going to have to be removed, where the crib will be situated. It's all real, until one day it's not.

I wondered if, even prayed that, one day Christine and I would have a baby—just *one*—to sing to sleep, to read to, to drag to grocery stores while they wail in pure terror for no apparent reason.

Still, because of this entire experience, if Christine said to me, "I don't want to try again," I wouldn't have fought her on it. We had talked about having children since before we got engaged, but the desire had been rung out of me like spit-up from a cloth bib. I couldn't stop asking myself, "What if this happens again? Or what if nothing happens?"

The problem is . . . opportunities don't linger; you'll miss them if you sit and wait, or take time feeling sorry for yourself. I wasn't brave enough to make that decision on my own. But Christine was.

We embraced in the entryway of our home after Christine's final visit with her OB/GYN. Then we stepped back, and Christine looked at me and said, "We're not done." I just nodded.

The problem is . . . we *couldn't* know what would happen next. We'd be taking a chance again.

The problem is . . . I wanted something but not the adversity.

The problem is . . . I'm willing to miss out on a good thing if it means *maybe* avoiding something bad altogether.

The problem is . . . weakness. The problem is fear. The problem is doubt.

The solution is . . . my wife, because if it weren't for her, I wouldn't be able to hold the most adorable son on the planet every day, listen to him laugh, sing to him, read to him . . . wrestle him until both tiny arms are through the sleeves of his onesie.

Life isn't a roulette wheel, and I shouldn't treat it like a gamble. The problem is . . . no one should.

CLAP WHEN I SAY SO

I have gone three decades without ever learning how to change the oil in a car. In my defense, I was a child during a lot of that time. Come to think of it, I don't even know exactly when I grew up and became an adult. All I know is that one day I wasn't ordering off the kids menu anymore, even though I still wanted chicken fingers and fries.

I figured I could easily learn to change my car's oil by watching a tutorial on YouTube, but every three thousand miles I convinced myself otherwise. By thirty years old, I've accepted that I'll never learn to change my own oil without asking someone else to teach me. There's a lot I'll never learn without first asking for help, like installing recessed lighting, changing a ribbon on a typewriter, or embalming a corpse. Oil changes top that list. But grown men don't go around asking other grown men and women how to do something as simple as replenishing the motor oil in a vehicle. So since that is out of the question,

I've resolved that paying considerable fees for the service every few months is a more logical option.

I've spent many mornings in dank and wary waiting rooms while mechanics worked on my car. The trouble was that you had to trust these men and women, because you usually couldn't see them while they worked. They'd have your car for *at least* twenty minutes every visit. That's plenty of time to hide a tracking device behind your radiator support or dump a bag of garter snakes in your glove compartment. The likelihood of either of those scenarios happening was slim—or, arguably, nonexistent—but your mind wanders while you're sipping on day-old coffee and perusing two-year-old women's health magazines when you'd forget to bring a book. The truth is, I trust these people with my car more than I trust myself with it. So I'll tolerate any waiting room for that kind of peace of mind.

Some mechanic shops dress up their lobbies attractively: a warm ambiance molded through careful interior design. These rooms don cushioned seats, flat-screen TVs, and fancy coffee machines that make one serving at a time. The temperature is always as crisp as an apple orchard in October, and you'd easily forget that hundreds of different types of chemicals and grease sit just on the other side of the wall, ready to explode from one rogue spark.

Other shops don't try to hide the fact that they have no time to worry about interior design. They were in business for their ability to fix cars, not renovate sitting rooms. Their waiting areas resemble patient quarters in those abandoned hospitals where teenagers have séances or orgies or whatever they do—I don't know; I was never invited. The seats in these types of waiting rooms are usually folding chairs, rusted through by sweat and body odor. And the dusty Sony portables hang in the corner of the room against the ceiling, fastened to the wall only by thin black metal clasps. The televisions never have remote controls, so you're forced to watch whatever staticky program is barely channeling in. Otherwise, in order to reach the buttons on the face of the TV, you'd have to risk breaking your neck by straddling a decomposing folding chair.

Nearly a decade ago, I was sitting in one of these folding chairs in one of these shops, when a mechanic shouted at me, "You need an oil change!" His voice was just loud enough that I heard it over a car backfiring in his lot, but it didn't make me look up from Mary Shelley's *Frankenstein* lying open on my lap. After a few seconds, he shouted again, "You need an oil change!" I clapped my book shut, forgetting to put the bookmark in place first, and looked up at him. Then he added, "Well, not you. Your car."

My mechanic, Lou, was a burly man, his XL T-shirt wrinkled everywhere except around the bulge of his belly. He seemed to have a perpetual tan, as if instead of fluorescent lights in his garage he used tanning bulbs in every socket. No matter what reason he was stepping out of his garage—to greet a visitor, take a call, yell at a customer—he always held a greasy, once-white rag in his hand.

He also had this uncomfortable habit of staring at you just a little too long before departing, as if he were awaiting some sort of applause. It was especially peculiar when you considered that mechanics typically try to escape you, not hang around longer and chat.

I wasn't at Lou's shop that day for an oil change. My car—Lemon, as I called her—needed serious servicing, but neither Lou nor I could figure out what that was. Lemon was nearly two decades old, a tan '96 Mercury Mystique, passed down to me by my grandparents a few years prior. The model car was discontinued years before Ford eventually dissolved Mercury altogether. Even *they* knew it was no more useful for drivers than a Playskool wagon with a steering wheel.

Lemon had failed inspection twice in the past two months, something about an unreadable On-Board Diagnostics system. I pretended to know what that meant, but not even Google could help me. As far as I could find, my car definitely had an On-Board Diagnostics system, but what that did was beyond me. I didn't feel as bad about my ignorance when even Lou couldn't figure it out after a couple visits, and he'd been in this business for at least forty years. He did know that my car needed an oil change this time, so I told him, "Go ahead." Then, after a six-second pause, he retreated to the garage, wiping his hands with his signature rag.

A couple years after Lou's garage moved three towns over, I found another local mechanic shop just like his. The receptionist's desk was next to the waiting area, elevated like a judge's stand in court. I sat on a brown folding chair by the window, surrounded by a crowd of blue folding chairs. On the other side of me was a square folding table typically used as a platform on which seniors play cards. It held a stack of paper cups and a Mr.

Coffee caked with crust around the handle and buttons.

In the far corner of the room hung a twenty-two-inch TV-VCR, playing some daytime cooking show. I was somewhat startled by the studio audience erupting into a deafening applause that made the TV go staticky for a moment. It wasn't even a competitive cooking show, so I wasn't expecting to hear an ovation for the chef running the program. She had just completed a pasta dish. It was difficult to see between bursts of static, but the linguini she served was drenched in pesto, which is essentially puréed basil. I enjoy pesto as much as the next Italian-American, but her dish looked only marginally better than mine. My pesto and linguini looks like grated crabgrass over strings of a mop. I give it a fancy name, though, so that it sounds aristocratic, or at least dignified. It's known as "Pasta di Spago Verdeggiante" in my house, which translates to "pasta of verdant string." I wouldn't serve it to guests, and I certainly wouldn't suggest it appear on cable television. But part of the culinary enterprise must be confidence, something I'm not known to have in abundance.

As soon as the host placed the plate of pasta on the counter in front of her, the audience felt the need to cheer. Moments later, the host reached into the on-set oven and pulled out a tray of brownies—or, technically, one giant brownie until it was cut. As soon as she placed the tray on the set's stove, the audience erupted again, as if their idol had just hit a walk-off home run or bench pressed six hundred pounds. I couldn't figure the purpose behind cheering when someone finished cooking a meal, but I somehow understood it. Few of life's necessities can top food, and a well-cooked meal deserves praise, but that nor-mally comes *after* one has tried the meal, not as soon as one sees it. So many things look great but are actually terrible. Think of any of your exes, and you'll know what I mean.

Still, this woman was receiving applause for every edible item she flaunted, and that felt unwarranted. After all, how many sons and daughters cheer when their mothers place meat-loaf on the kitchen table—or even a rack of tender baby back ribs? When my dad made my brothers and me burgers on the grill, I never clapped, unless I wanted to get smacked on the back of the head. My mother has made me more meals than I could name during my lifetime; not once did I slap my hands together in elation.

The more I thought about it though, the more I liked it. Why not applaud for the completion of a meal? In the United States, nothing is praised as much as food, although Americans only cheer for it during hot-dog-eating contests. Perhaps this trend should be followed well beyond the preparation of meals. We clap at sporting events, at concerts, and at the conclusions of speeches. It's a fundamental way in which one shows appre-ciation. So who's to say this act is unsuitable during everyday occurrences? I wouldn't mind a round of applause whenever I carry an entire trunk's worth of groceries into the house. Instead, I'm told, "Pat, you're going to hurt yourself! And I'm not taking you to the hospital when you do!"

It wouldn't be long before the clapping loses its significance, though. You don't chronically clap for the same reason you don't tell your significant other "I love you" every few minutes: it's annoying and starts to sound weird after a while.

The same goes for participation trophies. Older folks believe that distributing awards to kids who haven't technically won anything creates generations of egotistical maniacs who thirst for accolades every time they fart. However, participation trophies alone can't do that. What they've really done is obliterate the prestige of awards. Most of us who received participation trophies growing up don't give a crap about any special distinctions now, because we know they're worthless. That's what would happen, I suppose, if we started clapping for everything, too.

You may tell a temperamental friend to pick his battles; you'd likely say the same to someone who claps whenever a delivery man brings a package to the front door. Before long, cheering would evolve beyond just clapping and whistling. Soon, parents would bring air horns to graduation ceremonies in order to truly express their pride for an advancing dependent. That'd be stronger and much more deafening than banging one's hands together, and it would suppress all other forms of ovation. That's called Darwinism, I believe.

As I sat in this mechanic's waiting room, I continued to watch the cooking show on the TV, internally debating the cultural mores of frequently clapping.

Before cutting her brownies, the host covered them in a layer of powdered sugar. Her audience went wild, and I, an onlooker from thousands of miles away, had the urge to stand up and begin applauding, too. Remaining quiet in my rickety folding chair would only confirm that I was not ready to cultivate the societal changes that appear inevitable. Regardless, I stayed silent in my seat, but I told myself that the next time someone cooked me a meal or lent me a DVD, I'd applaud.

The show host received one last ovation before breaking for commercials when the mechanic's receptionist broke me from my trance. "Mr. Lombardi," she said, "your car's done. You're all set."

I wasn't sure if this was my opportunity, but my body didn't give my brain much time to decide. Impulsively, I slapped my hands together once and kept them embraced for a second. Then I separated them, ready to crack down into a subsequent clap.

This is only the beginning.

NICE NICE BABY

As soon as a baby's born, relatives begin comparing him to the parents. Somehow, people believe that the porcelain, mouse-like features of a newborn are comparable to the greasy, pulpous lineaments of a fully grown person. The baby may still be dripping mucus and afterbirth, fresh out of his mother's womb, yet adults are convinced he has his father's feet.

Babies are fascinating little creatures, I admit. They're smart, even months before they speak their first words. They're strong, even when they can't support their own heads. And they're hilarious, even if they eat less than a rodent yet poop as much as a woolly mammoth. Babies are living contradictions, and that's the most interesting thing about them—so I'd ask a hundred better baby-related questions before wondering who an infant resembles. However, I'm in the minority.

If you were to walk through the maternity ward in any North American hospital, you are guaranteed to hear relatives assigning traits to respective parents. "Aw, wittle Jamie is such a peanut when she sleeps," Grandma Jo might mutter. "She has her mommy's nose, lips, chin, and hands, and daddy's ears, forehead, knuckles, and chubby cheeks . . . May I prop open her eyes to confirm they're daddy's as well?"

It's a mystery to me why paternity tests still exist. Three middle-aged women from New Jersey can confirm a baby's lineage with one hundred percent accuracy, and the only forms of compensation they require are lotto scratch-offs and a carton of Parliament Silver Blue. If these women ever began advertising, they'd shut down paternity testing at LabCorp, which is only 99.99 percent accurate.

Everyone in my family enjoys comparing babies to their parents, and I'm sure everyone in your family does as well. I, too, do get a certain satisfaction in telling my friend that he and his son have the same chops. It's nearly a professional sport. The task requires the same adeptness, concentration, and confidence as, say, football or hockey. It won't be long until Marie from Atlantic City and Tony from Bayonne are on the covers of *Sports Illustrated* and *USA Today Sports Weekly*. Instead of holding footballs and hockey sticks, they'll tuck swaddled newborns under their chests, Heisman style. They can attribute every characteristic trait of a baby to each parent better than Tom Brady can toss a football.

One could argue that this sort of behavior strips a child of their individuality; something always belongs to one parent or the other, and there is nothing that the kid has developed on their own. However, just like any good sport, this one never ceases in the face of controversy. In reality, it thrives on it. Grandpa George isn't going to stop calling his grandson by his son's name, because they're practically one and the same. Aunt Tracey is still going to stare at you, even when you demand she stop, and then say you scold just like your mother. This conduct from relatives may be more natural than childbirth itself. I'm beginning to believe the whole reason babies are conceived is so they can be compared to someone from the moment they exit the womb.

Needless to say, this behavior has gotten out of hand. While it's foolish to continuously compare a baby's traits and actions to the parents, I'm just waiting for the day that an elderly man is told he has his father's silvery locks or that he has wrinkled just like his mother had. Sure, maybe it's true, but I've yet to be smacked by a lazier form of conversation. Where does it *end*? It's science, people! Daddy's sperm fertilized Mommy's egg like Scotts Turf Builder on Kentucky bluegrass. Within nine months, we're evicted from our first apartment for never making rent and we meet the world—half mother, half father (give or take).

Yes, your son likely does sneeze as loud as his mom, and your daughter probably does slap like her dad. You're applauded—not by me, but by someone—for your astuteness in catching such similarities. But there are more pressing matters at hand, such as: How in the world did this baby shit out of his diaper?

ROAD RAGE

The left lane is for speeding; the right lane is for daydreaming. That should be taught in driver's ed, but it's conveniently left out of the curriculum and absent from the DMV's website. During the four hours spent waiting in line to renew our driver's licenses, an employee should come around and shout unwritten rules of the road at us. It's the least they could do—so that I'm not stuck behind some student driver in the left lane when I'm already running late for work.

I'm afraid to find out if OnStar records at all times, because what I shout at other drivers should never be heard by human ears. Simply put: I loathe commuting. The mere term alone—*commute*—makes my blood boil. I almost refuse to speak the word aloud, because it leaves a bitter taste in my mouth for the rest of the day, and not even Listerine or turpentine can banish it. No matter what profanity you've heard me mutter, "commute" is by far the worst. I have no sympathy or patience for anyone or anything on the road. Perhaps I was spoiled as a kid, when early three-dimensional video games gave a taste of what driving a car *should* be like.

At about eight years old, I used to run across the street to my friend's house to hang out. We'd get into all sorts of trouble '90s kids found themselves in—ding-dong ditch, prank phone calls—but mostly we'd just play football, basketball, and baseball, and watch *Pokémon*. Oftentimes, we would sneak down to his partially finished basement and power up his first-generation Sony PlayStation 2. Video games were still relatively new and mystical, but even though he owned a couple dozen different games, we only played one: *Grand Theft Auto III*. It was a third-person action-adventure sandbox game where simple cheat codes punched into the controller could get you a rotary cannon with infinite ammunition so you could blow off people's limbs. You could do virtually anything in these *Grand Theft Auto* games if you had cheat codes: change the weather, speed up time, cause riots, trample a cyclist with a sedan and not get arrested.

Adults at the time were insistent that children who played these games would become violent and incorrigible, as if they'd go to bed fluffy Mogwais one night and wake as reptilian gremlins the next morning. Concerned parents were convinced we'd devolve into bloodthirsty malefactors dead set on accelerating the degradation of society as they knew it. It sounded like they were afraid we'd take the jobs away from politicians sooner than expected.

All *Grand Theft Auto* did for me was give unreal expectations of driving. I mean, I knew the actual operation of a motor vehicle was going to be more difficult than holding down X on a PlayStation controller, but I thought traffic actually flowed, for instance, which turned out to be rare. Unlike in the video games, I can't pass vehicles on double-yellow lines, run red lights, push cars with the front of my pixelated SUV, or smash roadside payphones and watch the excited gray particles of debris cascade like confetti around my somehow undamaged vehicle. There's no autonomy on U.S. roadways, and it's an epidemic.

I've become skeptical of road workers. I suspect they largely don't even start some of the jobs they're required to do. When you pull up to a roadwork area, there are flaggers halting traffic, displaying their oversized stop signs like an underachiever shows off a C-minus to his parents. But once he flips the sign to *Slow* and you crawl through the "work zone," I implore you to take a look around. I often see men sitting in the beds of their trucks, either biting their nails or fiddling with their cell phones. I rarely hear drilling or any other noises that indicate manual labor, and when I do hear those sounds, I'm confident it's only a recording blaring through the truck's stereo system, mimicking the type of roadwork that occurs in other countries.

Maybe they'll even scatter some debris near the road's shoulder so that when you find a nail in your flat tire, like I have, you figure there must have been some type of work going on.

If I had to guess, I'd assume these guys are the ones who have rigged our traffic light system. I'm convinced that the lights are designed to turn red whenever they sense my car approaching. Until I started driving, I never realized that traffic lights were actually demonic checkpoints designed to delay your commute by three minutes at every stop. They don't prevent vehicle collisions any more than surveillance cameras prevent thefts. This isn't some wild conspiracy theory, as I'm sure you experience it, too. The same stale green lights always turn yellow when I'm just too far away to rush through them. Sometimes they're generous and leave the light green just long enough for me to legally and safely cross the intersection, but those incidents are few and far between, and sometimes I find myself slowing down as I approach the intersection, because I've forgotten what it's like to *not* stop at a traffic light. I can't help but believe that is all part of the "design." It's ingenious, really, but perhaps not as ingenious as the faux school buses headed nowhere. They rival the bumbling tractor trailers that make it their mission to cut you off then kick up stones with their gargantuan tires and dent your hood or crack your windshield, which also has happened to me. School buses are bad omens. They're the black cats of vehicles. As soon as you see one, you know your commute is doomed.

In various parts of New Jersey, and likely the United States, I believe there are random men who own decommissioned school buses. They pick up no students and consequently drop none off. One of these men was a stain on my morning commute twelve months out of the year. I'd get stuck behind him driving fifteen miles per hour under the speed limit through three towns in two different counties every single morning. No matter how early I left, I still couldn't get past him. Then he'd veer right, and I'd forget all about him as I'd slow down for another red light.

If I'm not stopping at a red light or at the insistence of an overly confident flagger, I'm slowing down so that I don't rear end someone who just cut me off. In theory, the person cutting me off should be in a rush and should be speeding through neighborhoods. In reality, he drives as slowly as a school bus, and I know I'll be late for work. In these instances, I watch my clock race my speedometer, and the clock always wins. I often contemplate abandoning my car and running the rest of the way to work, which undoubtedly would be quicker. Instead, I wallow in the traffic and admire the glimmering crack on my windshield.

Just beyond that crack, I can see any cyclists who are daring enough to chance a New Jersey roadway during rush hour. They often are ignorant to sidewalks and paved bike paths and prefer to ride slowly in the middle of the road. It's possible that they may *want* to be hit by a car. I imagine they're seeking some type of disability pay. But as I watch each driver ahead of me dodge the cyclist, I follow in their skid marks and leave the cycling daredevil in my rearview mirror, only to contemplate taking him out another day.

You probably think I'm being harsh. My hatred for commuting oozes out of me like gasoline from a defective pump. I've become blind to the beautiful scenery that governs the anonymous countryside of the Garden State, because my eyes are drawn to the shredded black pavement and rolling machinery that plague it. Maybe you don't agree with my assessments. You don't have to take my word for it. I've endured a myriad of commutes for a measly dozen or so years, but I haven't fully enveloped myself in the majesties of this complex infrastructure. Perhaps I've just filled my head with fallacies that only help to make my commute more unbearable. Instead of picking out the pleasures of driving, I've presented a one-sided view of why sometimes I wish I had repeatedly failed my driving test. Sure, it gets me to Wendy's and the bookstore, but, overall, driving sucks.

Most of my commute is spent shouting the speed limit at the drivers in front of me, who are driving slower than allowed and couldn't hear me regardless. I wish my car horn was a blaring "HURRY UP!" Then I certainly would get more use out of it.

I think I'm on the road too much—or, somehow, not enough. I spent much of my youth virtually navigating the streets of Liberty City, Vice City, and San Andreas inside the fuzzy resolution of a twenty-two-inch Samsung television set. I don't think it made me a more violent person, though. The most aggressive thing I've ever done was threaten an HP Pavilion laptop with a flurry of profanity that would be bleeped out on daytime television yet conversationalized on HBO. Still, I have my savage fantasies. No amount of counseling would terminate them, especially not the ones I have while driving. They're therapeutic, even nostalgic.

One evening during my commute home from a particularly stressful day at work, I curved around a wooded bend that opened up to a wide forty-five mile-per-hour throughway, open fields on either side of the road. On the right, about a quarter mile down, was a green farmhouse, the driveway a paved, meandering zigzag, like something out of *The Wizard of Oz*. At the end of this driveway I saw a big-screen TV against the curb. It was one of those projection sets from the early 2000s, bulky and cumbersome like a Victorian-era armoire with Botox. It looked larger and larger beyond my cracked windshield as I approached it. And I just wanted to tilt my steering wheel to the right and slam my car right into it, *Grand Theft Auto*-style, and watch as the confetti of debris exploded around my undamaged car.

But I drove past the TV without smashing it—and, realistically, my car. *Not this time*, I thought. Maybe I'll wait for a cyclist.

DO NOT DISTURB

When I had my own office—before I got promoted and was downgraded to a cubicle—I considered booby-trapping my doorway. I wasn't sure how one went about booby trapping *anything*, let alone a place of business, but I came up with a dungeon's worth of promising quagmires. They'd all work way more effectively than a do-not-disturb sign, which doesn't do the job it's prescribed to do. Might as well hang a FREE FOOD IN HERE notice on the door.

I knew that I didn't want an aggressive booby trap or anything remotely dangerous. I'd rather "send a message." I wasn't looking for anything that could get me fired, arrested, or, perhaps worst of all, sued. I just needed to make it clear that my office wasn't an orientation center, nor was it an inbox for "shit that needs to get done right now."

I feared that I had become a magnet for people who needed mundane tasks completed. Most colleagues felt comfortable coming to me with any questions or issues that could have easily been answered by Google, which, frankly, has a much better track record than I do.

When I first started in my old office, there was no support staff. Well, there was one assistant, but she'd show up to work, clip coupons, go home, rinse and repeat, every day. Even though I didn't fill this void, some coworkers believed I had nothing better to do than scan their documents, schedule their meetings, and bring their boxes of files to the attic. For some reason, I always said yes, and thus initiated an endless cycle in which they never stopped asking me for help.

I twice had to teach a sixty-something-year-old about the Caps Lock key on a computer keyboard, emphasizing that he should never use it for any correspondence. He still continued to use it exclusively for emails. If that *was* part of my professional responsibilities, then I blame myself for not taking a closer look at the job posting when I applied.

There were times when I would go days without being asked how to indent a paragraph in Word, but once I started to sink in my own paperwork and timely reports, the bidding poured in. A coworker would approach my office door without greeting and request my immediate action, whether it be sending a fax, mailing a letter, or working a telephone.

None of these devices or services are new. They didn't just spring into existence at the start of the fiscal year. They all had been around before I was even born, which makes me wonder how some of my coworkers ever got by without me. I'm no genius or intellectual by any stretch, and there are tons of people who work harder and smarter than I do. That only compounds my colleagues' helplessness. Maybe I should be thankful that I never was sent on a coffee run, but nonetheless, it's like a lifeguard tossing me a rebuilt transmission while I'm treading the sea and then shouting, "Don't get that wet!"

I know many others who feel this way, which is why I planned to patent the booby trap once I invented it. I'd be an entrepreneur *and* a humanitarian.

I'd start by giving it a snappy name. That's what'll get it the most attention. Like Station Liberation, Area Barrier, or Compass Rumpus. The name should rhyme—it'd seem less hazardous that way. Once I figure out what to call it, then I can get into the mechanics.

The contraption may need some type of sensor, which will distinguish the welcomed guests from the tiresome intruders. After all, the last thing you'd want is to shoo away the smiling faces of those who don't make inane requests regularly. They offset the bothersome coworkers. There's a balance that needs to be maintained, and I'm not about to ignore that. The consequences could be calamitous. Conversationalists bearing gifts should be saluted, not blasted in the buttock with a fast-acting tranquilizer dart. (Don't worry, I'm just throwing ideas out there to see what sticks. My prototype is far from ready.)

In an ideal world, the aforementioned sensor would swiftly detect those employees who are determined to pass their responsibilities onto you. You know who I'm talking about: the people who have time to harass you to get their tasks done but too little time to get the tasks done themselves. If they have time to complain that they're *so busy*, they likely have plenty of time to get all of their work completed and then see an opera with the remaining hours. Still, they have no qualms about passing work off onto another employee.

There were times they even smirked at me and questioned my understanding. "You know how to do this, right?" I've been asked before. And since I would've felt like a fool to turn them away at this point, I'd tell them yes as I snatched away their chores. Their time, or lack thereof, is somehow always more valuable than anyone else's.

My booby trap's sensor, therefore, would need to detect the speed and manner in which these individuals walk, or perhaps the contents they hold in their hands. When people are on a mission to dump some work on you, they hardly blend into their surroundings. They're often carrying packets of files stuffed into over-stretched manila folders. My proprietary invention would catch and demobilize them instantaneously. As they approach your office door, a red light would flare up, an alarm would sound, and a giant flyswatter would descend from the ceiling and whack the papers from their fists. It wouldn't stop swatting until the perpetrator was a safe distance away. I'm thinking at least a hundred feet.

The booby trap would have an everlasting effect, as your coworkers would never forget the terror that had befallen them the last time they tried to get you to do something irrelevant to your responsibilities. This is true innovation. Now I know how Eli Whitney felt.

There's no reason to live and work *without* booby traps. Simply closing your office door is about as effective as putting a "Kick Me" sign on a soccer ball. It's never taken seriously. So the only way to avoid these beggars is to actively defend against them. A lasso that wraps around the ankles and hangs them upside-down from the ceiling, a trap door that sends them careening down a dark tube slide into a basket of laundry in the basement, a *Men in Black*-type device that wipes their recent memory clean so they forget why they came to your office space in the first place—all of these would provide you with the peace of mind you've been craving since you accepted your first full-time office position.

Maybe it's not professional, but it needs to be done. I don't see another more logical or viable solution. Think about all of the work that would get completed efficiently across the nation if laborers focused on the tasks at hand rather than which duties can be passed off to someone else.

Our country was built by men and women who fought in the fields and trenches alongside their people. I'd like to believe that these same men and women could've at least operated a fax machine without any assistance if the opportunity presented itself. Ultimately, isn't that the American Dream—to be independent and unregimented? That's *my* American Dream. Well, that, and also making a boatload of money from an office booby trap.

WHERE DID YOU GO TO CULINARY SCHOOL?

Don't look for people who are passionate about food trucks. We'll find *you*. We're a kooky bunch and maybe not as much fun as you might think.

I used to cover food trucks for an online series, and so it was difficult not to fall in love with the cuisine. I'm American, after all. Unfortunately, I'm a somewhat picky eater. I hate that I am, but I sucked it up for that job. I couldn't keep covering the same types of trucks over and over again. People need their options. Just because I'm not a vegan and don't gravitate toward Thai food doesn't mean there isn't an audience out there for either. I used this job to push me out of my comfort zone, try food I wouldn't normally eat, put myself in my readers' shoes.

Give them *variety*. Like a pothole on the freeway, I opened myself up to the point of discomfort.

Most food trucks specialize in one area of food, be it barbecue, cheesesteaks, burgers, pizza, chicken, meatballs, or even eclectic comfort food. It's something that defines them. The reign of the questionable lunch trucks has given way to gourmet food trucks. There are festivals dedicated just to these culinary connoisseurs serving straight from the orifices of their decadent mobile rigs. A lot of the events are packed with guests, regardless of the weather or time of year. It's a whole new industry finally birthing in the Garden State and beyond.

Several years ago, I encountered one food truck that specialized in seafood and also burgers and also chicken tenders and also those fried potatoes with smiley faces cut out of them. Occasionally, the menu would offer barbecue, and other times it'd offer warm desserts served à la mode. I couldn't pinpoint exactly what kind of truck this was, and I also couldn't find a single photo of it online. My editor had suggested I set something up with this truck, but neither of us had any solid info on the business.

Its name was Piranha Trap, a notion that surely gets those salivary glands pumping. I scheduled a meeting with the owner, Terri, at a fundraiser for an elementary school in South Plainfield. We agreed that 10:30 A.M. would be the perfect time to squeeze in an interview and to take some photos of her truck and her food before the event started at eleven.

I parked my car in the school's front lot at 10:30 on the dot, and I nearly sprinted into the schoolyard, where parents in red T-shirts were managing the event. One stopped me to see if I was all right.

"Just late for an interview with a food truck," I told him.

"You're interviewing a *truck*?" he asked, giggling. "Is KITT's brother out there?" He chortled at his dad-joke reference to *Knight Rider*, and I thought he was about to choke to death.

"Yeah, actually," I told him. "And he likes punctuality, so I better . . ." I scooted past him, though he hardly noticed through his tears of joy.

When I stepped out onto the school's playground, I could see the entire spread of food trucks and crafts and games vendors. I scanned the field but didn't see Piranha Trap. I had no idea what the truck even looked like, so I studied each one individually and read their names aloud. Seven trucks, but no Piranha Trap. I did a lap around the school and checked the parking lot, but still couldn't find her.

At 10:40 A.M., I felt it appropriate to put out an A.P.B. for Terri. The event was starting in twenty minutes, and she hadn't had any time to prep yet, let alone take time for an interview.

I might be at the wrong event, I thought. But when I checked my email on my phone, I saw that, no, I was at the right place, or at least at the place where Terri told me she would be. So I walked up to a red-shirted woman holding a walkie-talkie. She was consoling a five-year-old, who had dropped his fidget spinner in the dirt, and now it looked like a relic from an aberrant futuristic society.

"Excuse me," I interrupted. "Is Piranha Trap supposed to be here today?"

"Oh, yes," she replied, wiping the fidget spinner on her hip. "We've been waiting for her. She hasn't called and hasn't answered her phone. Do you know where she is?"

"No, I'm waiting for her, too. We were supposed to meet at 10:30 for an interview."

The woman told me she'd let me know if she heard anything. "In the meantime, feel free to hang out, enjoy the other food trucks, make some crafts." She knelt down and handed the boy his fidget spinner. He started crying once he noticed there still was some dirt in its crevices.

I walked away and sat on a bench in the center of the enormous half-circle of food trucks and vendors. I scanned the present trucks a third time. I knew that Piranha Trap still wasn't here, but the event did garner trucks I recognized and enjoyed. There was a lobster-roll truck, a burger truck, and my favorite cheesesteak truck, one I had covered the previous season. It was a business run by a husband-and-wife team. Every element of their cheesesteak was scrutinized, including the homemade cheese for the steaks.

I walked up to their truck, where the wife Donna was working. After greeting each other, she asked, "What are you doing here today? Covering another truck?"

"Yeah, Piranha Trap," I told her. "But she's still not here yet. No one has any idea where she is."

Donna looked down at her watch. "Well, she better get moving. Event started ten minutes ago. Some event planners won't even let you on grounds if you're late." I nodded but didn't say anything. At this point, I wasn't even sure I wanted to meet Terri. I've been forty minutes late before, but she's two hours and ten minutes late to this event, in food-truck time, and didn't try to get in touch with anyone or even answer her phone. I hoped she was not in a medical emergency or involved in some other tragedy, but I had a feeling that wasn't the case.

Then Donna interrupted my thoughts. "Are they looking for you?" She pointed to a group of three ladies in red shirts about a hundred feet away. One was holding a walkie-talkie and pointing in our direction. Then she motioned to the back of the field, where a blue box truck was parking behind the last food truck in line.

I turned to Donna. "That must be Piranha Trap," I said. "I'll talk to you in a bit."

"Stop by before you leave if you're still hungry," she told me. "I'll hook you up with a garlic bread cheesesteak."

I smiled and waved and headed toward Piranha Trap. From far away, it appeared to be a moving van painted with waves and splashing water. Food trucks are sometimes trailers, which latch onto the back of a vehicle to be pulled. However, they're always outfitted to serve food, even if they're converted from another type of truck. They typically have a large window on one side and underneath is a ledge with condiments, napkins, utensils, and awards, if the truck has won any. From there, owners will get creative. Maybe they'll have a television on the side so patrons can watch sports while at a festival or a catered event. Some have speakers for music. Most have specialty wraps with their logos and names proudly displayed no matter what angle of the truck you see.

As I approached Piranha Trap, I realized that it was neither a trailer nor a traditional food truck. It was a Class-3 light-duty box truck, roughly twelve feet long. We had just used one of these to move Christine and her dad out of their old house. It's tighter inside the back cab than it appears from the outside. You could fit a dresser, a couple nightstands, a short hutch, and maybe a flat-screen or two, along with a dozen or so boxes, but good luck getting even a futon in there after all that.

I walked closer to Piranha Trap. On the side of the truck, someone had cut out a square about two feet by two feet. It was closed up from inside the truck by what looked like white poster board. The name PIRANHA TRAP was printed above the window in a basic sans-serif font, likely Arial. Underneath the window was a picture of one solitary piranha. I think his name might've been Trap, but I forgot to ask. Next to Trap, barely legible, was a tag identifying the vehicle as a food truck. The entire vehicle was one shade of royal blue and wrapped with a beach-y design, but if you saw this thing barreling down the highway, you'd think someone was moving down the shore, or possibly living in the back. Your first impression wouldn't be that it serves food.

I walked to the back, where a woman with frizzy black hair

was lifting the truck door. "Yes, can I help you?" she asked.

"I'm Pat Lombardi," I responded. She stared at me and said nothing. "For the interview and photoshoot today." I held up my camera bag.

"*Oh*, yeah, yeah, that's right. I'm Terri." She stepped on a mechanical lift that carried her from the ground to the back of the truck. "I'm just getting set up now, but feel free to hang around until I'm done." She grabbed an orange traffic cone out of the back of the truck. It had the letters UWJC printed on the side. I later learned that those letters stand for "United Water Jersey City," meaning the cone formerly belonged to the municipality of Jersey City, New Jersey. Now it belonged to Piranha Trap. After picking up the cone, Terri grabbed a thick green pole with a banner that had only one word printed on it: SEAFOOD. So, Jersey City, if you've been searching for a missing orange traffic cone, it's been promoted to a banner holder, and it's not looking back.

Terri used the lift to get back down, walked to the side of her truck where Trap was, dropped the cone on the ground, and shoved the pole into the top hole. As the seafood banner waved in the breeze, Terri stopped and looked around at the trucks around her.

"Wow." She snickered. "They put me *right* next to a seafood truck. Of course." She waved a hand at me. "You can never depend on event organizers to care about you. As long as they're making money, that's all they care about. Now I have to compete with this food truck." She pointed her thumb at a red truck parked in front of hers. Its menu indicated it sold lobster rolls and French fries but nothing more. I wouldn't even classify it as a *shellfish* truck, let alone a seafood truck. But I kept those thoughts to myself, because I suspected Piranha Trap was no more a seafood truck than this other one.

"Maybe they just stuck you both at the end of the line because you were the last two to arrive," I offered. I don't know why I thought that would be a reassuring sentiment. Terri snorted but didn't add anything else. She walked to the back of the truck, and I followed. She again used the lift to bring her back into the truck. She was a thin woman and seemed very mobile. I was surprised she kept using the lift instead of hopping into the back of the truck, which couldn't have been more than two feet from the ground, maybe three. I don't know—I left my yardstick at home.

Terri grabbed a whiteboard, which was wedged underneath a dumbbell. The whiteboard had a list of food written on it in various colors. Terri held the board in her left hand and grabbed a hand towel from the floor with her right.

"Let's see what we have today," she said and glanced around the back of her truck. Then she individually erased items off what appeared to be the menu, leaving just fish tacos, shrimp tacos, mini cheeseburger sliders, and bourbon bacon scallops. It was a modest menu. Terri once again used the lift to get back off the truck. She leaned the whiteboard outside underneath the square service window, and she used the lift again to get back into the truck. Once she was inside, she said, "You can hop up here. I still have to prep, but I can do the interview while I get everything together."

I hopped onto the lift, next to a rumbling generator, and examined the back of her truck before taking a step inside. It was lined with beach-themed decorations and packed with kitchen appliances. The left wall was covered with two long blue shower curtains connected by scotch tape. Both curtains had the same cartoon sea creatures printed on them: dolphins, whales, turtles, and a collection of colorful fish. They didn't look real whatsoever, and I figured that was a running theme with this business. In front of the shower curtains were fishing nets held up by thumbtacks. Also on the left wall, Terri had installed a wire rack, which typically is found in bedroom closets and used to hang clothes and hide Christmas presents. Terri used hers to store burger buns, cooking utensils, and condiments.

Along the left and back walls was an L-shaped metal countertop, the kind you'd find in restaurant kitchens or prison mess halls. There were dried brown and black splotches on top that looked like the vacated cocoons of moths. It needed to be wiped down and disinfected, or altogether discarded. Instead, Terri used it in its current state to prepare food that she would serve to strangers. *Paying* strangers.

On the lower shelves below the countertop were cardboard boxes and plastic tubs. They were weathered and appeared filled from the outside, but I couldn't tell what was in a single one of them. Terri had some more boxes stacked around the back-right corner of the truck. The top one was discolored and leaking from the bottom. I wondered if that was where she kept the piranhas. Next to the stack of boxes was a microwave on its own stand, and next to that was a toaster oven. Another toaster oven sat on a stand at the end of the truck near the lift.

Terri dug through a box under the far side of the counter-top and pulled out a hot plate. "I thought I forgot this at home," she said, dropping it onto the countertop. She plugged the power cable into an extension cord on the floor.

While she continued to dig appliances and utensils out of various boxes, I pressed the record button on my tape recorder and placed it on the metal countertop in front of me. I didn't think now would be a good time to begin asking her questions, but I wanted to make sure this all was on tape. "Do you do this on your own?" I asked her.

"Oh yeah," she said, smirking. "I had a partner, but we had to go our separate ways. We just didn't have the same vision for this business." She pulled a bag of store-brand coleslaw from a cooler and slapped it onto the countertop in front of me. Then she reached for a bowl on top of the wire rack. "Also, we used to date. But we broke up before starting Piranha Trap. He was my boss when I was a bartender. We started culinary school together."

"Oh, where did you go to culinary school?"

"Yeah," Terri replied.

She picked a white bowl from the stack on top of the wire rack and placed it next to the bag of store-bought coleslaw. Then she snatched the bag and popped it open in one swift movement. "See, people love my coleslaw, because I make it like nobody else," she said, pouring the slaw into the white bowl. She pulled out a new jar of mayonnaise from under the counter, scooped two spoonfuls, and whacked them into the bowl, right on top of the slaw. She mixed the two together with the spoon and smiled at me. "Just prepping some now, because it's going to be a hot seller once guests start coming."

"So where did you go to culinary school?" I asked again.

"I went with my former partner, before he left the business." She tossed the bowl of coleslaw to the side, then walked over to the covered square window on the side of her truck. She ripped out the thumbtacks holding the poster board into place and dropped the poster board on top of the box that I suspected had piranhas inside. Then Terri turned to me. "Why don't I show you some of my dishes?" she said. "I make the best bourbon bacon scallops." She clapped her hands together and walked over to a mini refrigerator underneath the right side of the far counter. She opened it up and pulled out a saran-wrapped Styrofoam tray of a dozen scallops.

"That sounds good," I said, looking down at my tape recorder, which was still running. "Where are those from?"

"Restaurant Depot." Terri peeled the saran wrap off the top of the scallops and placed about five of them on the hot plate. She turned the device on high, covered the remaining scallops, and shoved them back into the mini fridge. "I make my own specialty bourbon sauce. It pairs so good with the scallops. People come back just for the sauce." She laughed and pulled out a bottle of Old Crow from a cardboard box underneath her metal counter. It had the pourer cap on the finish, as if she had lifted it straight from the bottom shelf of an Applebee's bar. She grabbed a small black paper ramekin from a plastic tub on the above wire rack and poured the bourbon inside. It was thin, no viscosity whatsoever. I wondered what she was going to mix it with, but she simply placed it down on the countertop and slid it in my direction.

Several feet from my face, it smelled like straight bourbon, no added ingredients to dilute it. It wasn't even *good* bourbon either. She went to the clearance section of the liquor store for this bottle. If *this* was the reason why people came back to Piranha Trap, I had no interest in trying her actual food.

Terri flipped the scallops over on the hot plate with plastic tongs I swear I've seen at the Dollar Tree. The cooked sides of the scallops were stiff and brown like tree bark. I knew that once she was done, I would have to be a good sport and eat them—or one at least. Maybe I could drop the rest on the floor, make it look like an accident, but that wouldn't be right. She spent her earnings on this food and was going out of her way to share it with me. Even if the food was atrocious, that's still a kind gesture.

She grabbed a paper Dixie plate from the wire rack and started spreading the scallops around the center of the plate. She took the ramekin of bourbon and placed it in between the scallops, then lowered the plate down in front of me and shouted, "Bon appétit!"

The scallops looked like burnt eyeballs. I thought maybe this was a dish she should wait until Halloween to serve. I snapped a couple photos of the dish with my Nikon, trying my best to make it look edible. Before I had a chance to pick which scallop I wanted, Terri snatched one off the plate, shoved it entirely into her mouth, and went back for a second. I picked one up on the far side of the plate, away from where she grabbed her first two, and I nibbled on it like a rabbit. It was tough and gamey, but I only worried a little that it would give me food poisoning. That was a good thing, I thought, though I certainly wasn't going back for a second.

"You didn't try the bourbon sauce!" Terri pointed out, although she didn't catch that it was a conscious decision. I dipped the non-bitten end of my scallop in the sauce and placed it on my tongue. It was straight bourbon, as I had suspected. This bourbon bacon scallop was suspiciously missing the bacon. You can't put a food item in a name if it isn't in the recipe. That has to be illegal.

I struggled to chew and swallow this offering, which really *was* starting to feel like an eyeball in my mouth. The bourbon only soured the flavor of the scallop; it didn't compliment it. I'm not much of a drinker, but Terri was right that I would want to come back for more of the "sauce" alone—I needed something to burn this flavor out of my mouth and throat. Turpentine would've worked as well. I felt like I had chewed on a playground woodchip.

"Mmm, tastes like sneakers and vomit," I thought to tell Terri. She didn't peg me for the type of person who easily had her feelings hurt. She wouldn't burst into tears if I spoke my mind, because she seemed more likely to press the sole of her shoe against my chest and literally kick me out of the back of her truck instead. Then she might go about her business, wondering how she could be the only person she's ever met who enjoys her cooking.

As I was chewing on the second half of my scallop, a guest came up to the window and ordered the shrimp tacos. I wanted to shoo her away, send her to the cheesesteak truck. "I know you're looking for seafood, but you won't find any here anyway, so why not just get a meaty cheesesteak?"

Terri took a box of SeaPak popcorn shrimp out of the mini fridge. She lifted the previously opened lip of the box and poured about six popcorn shrimp onto a metal tray. She pressed a couple buttons on the toaster oven next to her and shoved the tray inside. Terri then kneeled down and pulled two soft tortillas out of the cooler, slapped them onto another Dixie plate, and spread her *homemade* coleslaw all over their faces.

I thought about asking her more interview questions, but I needed at least another half hour to finish chewing this scallop; otherwise, she never would've clearly heard my inquiries. Incidentally, she was doing so much talking that I may not have been able to get a word in anyway.

"I don't know if this event is going to have a great turnout," she told me. "They promised hundreds of people would come out today. No, thousands—they told me thousands would come out today. I doubt that. The thing about food trucking is that most of the time your profit depends on the event organizer, who is supposed to promote the events. If they do a lousy job, you're making no money. They need to make sure they get a variety of trucks, too. There're *two* seafood trucks here today, which means we're splitting the business, splitting the money. Food trucking is a competition. We don't help each other. We're not pals. We have to look out for ourselves. Event organizers aren't going to do anything to help us."

The toaster oven dinged, and Terri took the shrimp out with a gray rag, tattered and damp, that she had sitting on the counter. She placed three shrimp in each coleslaw-filled tortilla. *She's going to charge that woman ten bucks for that?* I thought. I considered opening my mouth, but all that would've come out was bits of white rubber.

Terri handed her victim the shrimp tacos, snatched the ten-dollar bill out of her hand, and waved goodbye.

"*Oh,*" she rasped, with a sharp inflection in her voice, as if she was just told that her car insurance premium would be tripled. "I have to show you my lobster tail dish. This is a favorite. Nobody makes it like me. It's so different. I'm not selling it today, but I'll make one for you."

I hadn't noticed, but right in front of me, next to the counter, was a small cube freezer. Terri flipped open the lid and took out a lobster tail that was swathed by saran wrap.

"These are real, fresh lobster tails," she said proudly. I expected her to then beat her chest in victory. "My friend has a boat down the shore and catches lobster all the time." I had a feeling that wasn't his profession. I pictured a man standing at the back of a rowboat firing shotgun blasts into the water. I couldn't figure out, though, where in New Jersey lobsters were residing. But even if it is possible to catch and eat them, they can't be that good. I could be wrong here, but no one goes to a five-star restaurant and orders the New Jersey lobster. No one goes to *any* restaurant looking for it, for that matter.

While I was daydreaming, Terri had cut open the top of the lobster tail and placed it meat-side down on the hot plate, which, I just then realized, was never turned off after Terri finished brutalizing the scallops. "I picked up a lot of skills while at culinary school," Terri began.

"Where did you go to culinary school?" I inquired one more time, not really expecting a real answer.

"But certain things you just can't learn," she continued. "You either pick them up while cooking or you create them yourself. That's what I've done with my lobster tail." Terri grabbed another Dixie plate. "You're going to love this." Then she grabbed two skewers from a bin underneath the counter. She used the same tongs from before to lift the lobster tail from the hot plate and place it meat-side up on the paper plate. "I'm the only one who does this," Terri said while sliding one skewer vertically through each butterflied piece of lobster tail. When she was finished, it looked like the lobster tail had been brutally murdered by a team of pirates who had just finished roasting marshmallows.

Terri removed the plate of remaining scallops and placed the lobster tail down next to my tape recorder. I put my Nikon up to my eye and snapped some photos of the dish. Despite being served on a paper plate, it did actually look pretty appetizing. But I saw how it was prepared, and it didn't make my stomach growl. I changed angles a couple more times and snapped about another dozen or so shots. When I took the camera away from my eye, Terri pulled the dish away from me. "So we're done here?" she asked.

I hadn't finished the interview. I hadn't even gotten one straight answer from her. All I learned was that this is considered a food truck, her partner left, and she allegedly went to culinary school, but I wasn't even sure any of that was true. Still, I nodded and said, "Yes, we are."

I jumped off the lift of the box truck without saying another word. This was an abrupt conclusion to our meeting, a meeting for which the owner was nearly an hour late. Sometimes things just end a lot more suddenly than you'd anticipate. It's often a blessing, even if it doesn't feel that way. For example, I didn't get what I needed for my article, and now I was at risk of submitting something incomplete, thus ruining the ongoing series. However, if I had stayed longer, not only would I surely have been food poisoned or murdered, I may have had enough photos, quotes, and information to publish an article on a business I didn't want to tell people to support. I couldn't lie to my readers like that.

The series highlighted the *best* food trucks in the state. If this truck were featured in that series, I'd be sending people to a business that gets nearly one hundred percent of its meals from Walmart, something patrons can do themselves, without the three hundred percent upcharge. The best possible conclusion was that Terri shooed me away. I wasn't sure if she thought her constant complaining was enough to fill an entire article, or if she had second thoughts about being profiled alto-gether. Either way, I was thankful to be out of that moving truck. It was one hot plate away from exploding.

As I walked away from Piranha Trap, I noticed a line form-ing at the window five or six families deep. I took a step toward them, about to point them in the direction of any other food vendor at the event, but I couldn't actively undermine Terri's business. I didn't want to harm it any more than she already has. I decided against saying anything and continued to walk away from Piranha Trap and its newest prey. Then my stomach did something it hadn't done the entire morning, despite the fact that I had skipped breakfast: it growled. I started walking toward my favorite cheesesteak food truck.

When I had interviewed Donna and her husband the year before, they were warm and welcoming and open. I knew that neither of them went to culinary school, because they didn't pretend that they did. I helped to promote a family business that people loved and returned to regularly.

I wondered if Piranha Trap had any regular guests. There are masochists in the world, so there likely are people who'd enjoy Terri's food *and* attitude. Just because something isn't right for one person doesn't mean it isn't right for another.

There's a food truck industry blooming in the Garden State. It's good to know that at least we have our options.

THIS IS JANUARY'S

I made a New Year's resolution to write at least one creative, humorous piece a month for the entire year. The catch is that I have to start completely from scratch. Any journal entries, notes, or ideas I have written down before the beginning of each month are completely out of play. Nothing old or recycled. This is a feat for me, because while I write every day, not everything I write is meant to be funny. I have to allot time to get this done.

It's only the first month of the year, and already I feel like I'm in the kitchen with no ingredients.

So. This is it.

I probably should've given myself a word count.

UNEXPECTED PILFERING

Someone stole my pen. A *nice one*. I had been behind my booth at a street fair, failing to promote my first book. The event's organizers anticipated more than ten thousand attendees, and I hoped to gain the attention of just a fraction of them. This was the first event in which I had ever participated. I wasn't really sure what to expect, but theft certainly never crossed my mind. No one would want to steal a book, let alone *my* book. It had the word "junk" in the title, for crying out loud. And I expected people to pay money for it? I was over confident yet cripplingly insecure, somehow at the same time. That ought to be the Millennial's mantra.

I didn't anticipate much excitement or even anything noteworthy at this street fair. Yet, midway through the event, as I conversed with another vendor, an unknown woman approached the front corner of my booth. She eyed my books for a couple seconds. Then she grabbed one of my best gel pens, brimming with black ink, and slid it into her pants pocket. Without saying a single word, she slipped in and out, at least one pen richer than she had been when she entered the street fair.

A year after publishing my first book, I secured a vendor space at a street fair on an unfamiliar central New Jersey main street. It was the last full day of summer, when people started shying away from beaches and scoped fairs like these, looking for potential holiday gifts. The event predominantly featured painters, sculptors, wood workers, jewelry designers, and a slew of other creative types. The only kind of artist I didn't expect to see here were plastic surgeons, but, naturally, a local plastic surgeon had his own booth right between a graphic artist and a Korean barbecue food truck.

The presence of authors was scarce, but still I believed this event would be an appropriate place to sell copies of my first book. Surely once guests got bored of the extravagant artwork and one-of-a-kind jewelry, they'd be dying for something to read. I believe this type of false self-assurance is called "naiveté." But I figured if one percent of the visitors were interested in my book, I could sell about a hundred. Realistically though, I didn't think I'd get more than ten glances at my booth.

My debut book was relatively unrecognized. I titled it *Junk Sale* after one of the short stories in the collection. I'm not sure if the name improved or cost me sales, but I found the self-deprecating title fitting, even when my dad took one look at the proof copy and said, "*Really*, Pat? You couldn't think of a better title?"

Still, *Junk Sale* did receive positive feedback from the few people who had read it, mostly friends and family, who likely felt obligated to leave it zealous reviews. Regardless, I was slowly starting to accept that I wasn't just some self-diluted fool who self-published a book but instead considered myself an author who could potentially gain some momentum with his writing career. I forced myself to try events like this to see what could happen, and, with the exception of stepping in gum right at the front of my assigned booth, I was determined to embrace every part of it.

While setting up my tables and tent with Christine, who accompanied me the entire day, I was careful about the organization of my display. I was sure that posting a glowing newsletter article about me and my book would attract people, so I put it front and center. My former boss had written it when I first published *Junk Sale*. It was one of the few reviews written about the book, so I even provided copies of the article for anyone who was interested in free reading. I placed those next to promotional bookmarks, which lay in front of copies of my book, standing upright to show off an unimpressive book cover.

Before publishing the book—and even afterward—I regularly had internal battles about that cover. I wanted something that portrayed the essence of the book better, something more engaging and eye catching. The cover I stuck with was bland

and uninspiring. I have seen soccer balls with more pizazz, and those are made to be kicked around. This cover offered little insight as to what readers would discover once they opened the book. Still, I stuck with it; I had designed the cover artwork myself, and I didn't have deep enough pockets to pay a professional to do what I certainly couldn't. *It's what's on the inside that counts*, I figured. *Don't judge a book by its cover.* But I couldn't fool myself. Even *I* judge books by their covers. So I was sure that no reader would spend more than two seconds glancing at my product before skipping to the beautiful artwork in the booth next to mine.

Twenty minutes before the event started, visitors began filtering in. Neighbors who lived just outside the main street emerged from their homes and strolled through the street fair like zombies with no ambition to eat human brains.

Both sides of the street were lined with vendors, many of whom competed with each other to gain your business, though they wouldn't admit it. I didn't want to be the kind of vendor who's more focused on your wallet than on your enjoyment of a street fair. I couldn't summon the personality, or even the courage, to be a sufficient salesman. I wanted people to buy my book and hopefully take it home and read it, rather than discard it in the nearest trash bin. But I was positive that all the books I might sell that day, if any, would either rot on the buyers' shelves or find their way into donation boxes without ever being opened.

I stood at the front of my booth, awaiting someone to wander my way. I looked back at my display one last time to ensure that everything was neat and in proper order before people started ignoring my booth. I tapped the bookmarks, aligned the newsletter articles, and made sure all the books sitting on my table were uniformly stacked so that the binding faced outward. I even laid out an assortment of pens on the table in front of where I would be sitting, once I got tired of standing and greeting passersby.

When I looked up from my display, I saw a small woman walking toward me. She had short blond hair and black square, thick-rimmed glasses. She wore dark clothing and had a scarf tied around her neck, despite the temperature approaching the high eighties. She smiled and asked what I was selling.

"Just copies of my book," I mumbled, thinking this was one of the event's volunteers and not a potential customer. She looked down at my display, touched the pile of newsletter articles in front of her, and then grabbed a book and began flipping through it.

"Well, what's it about?" she asked, and I realized she didn't work or volunteer for the street fair. She was here for artwork and, evidently, literature.

"It's a collection of humorous short stories and essays. The first part of the book depicts interesting characters in everyday situations. The second part is about my experiences in life . . . working in a restaurant . . . living at home . . ." I let my voice trail off as she continued to flip through the book. I knew we were only seconds away from her putting it down and walking away. I wasn't even selling *myself* on the book. Had another author presented his work to me in this same manner, I would've considered him a somehow doubtful yet pompous ass and moved onto the next self-proclaimed artist. I wanted to say more about what I had written in this collection, but in my head, all of the content sounded silly.

My mom's obsessed with the freezer. Well, not really, but she uses it too much . . . Oh, a man finds love while committing burglary . . . And did I tell you how much I'm into indie music?

I kept my mouth shut. If she didn't buy the book, I didn't want it to be because I did a lousy job explaining how it's "humorous."

After a few moments of silence, she nodded and looked back up at me, still holding the book open with both of her hands. "What do you do for a living?" she asked. "Do you write a lot? What's your background?"

She hit me with three questions at once. I didn't know if I was being interviewed for a job or if this was how some people showed interest in a struggling independent author. I knew that two options existed: she either was going to leave my booth with a book or without one. So I decided to answer the questions how I wanted to, in a way I thought would result in a sale.

I pointed down to the pile of newsletter articles on the table next to us. "Full-time, I work for the State," I told her. "I graduated college with an English degree with a concentration in writing. From there, I did a lot of journalism and contract writing, and then I started with the State three years ago. I pretty much write nonstop. Most of my work is on BestofNJ.com—

lots of stuff about food trucks and traveling around the state."
I chuckled.

She didn't say anything at first and just nodded, trading views between me and the book in her hands. Then she tucked the book under her armpit and opened the satchel slung over her shoulder. "Why not? I'll give it a shot." She pulled a wallet from her bag, dug her hand inside, pulled out a twenty-dollar bill, and handed it to me. "I'd like to see what this is about." She smiled down at the book as I searched for change in my depleted wallet. When I found a ten-dollar bill, I handed it to her, and she said thank you, told me to have fun, and scurried away into a crowd of teenagers.

I was positive, right then in that moment, that this event was going to be worth it. The fair had not yet begun, and I already recorded one sale. Before the event was over, I reasoned I would be sold out of the sixty-odd books I had brought with me.

After neatly tucking the twenty into my wallet and stuffing the wallet into my back pocket, I decided to sit back down at my table. Visitors were going to come to *me*.

An hour then passed, and while people visited my booth, asked about the book, and took some bookmarks, no one else showed any interest in purchasing it.

I started talking to the vendor next to me in the second hour of the event. He was a woodworker in his free time, when he wasn't plumbing with his father-in-law. At the street fair, he was offering an eclectic collection of bird houses, jewelry boxes, coasters, chests, and end tables. I wanted to purchase one of his handmade creations, because he seemed like a nice guy, but I had no use for any of that stuff. If he was selling a coffin, at least then I'd be able to reason, "Well, I'll for sure need this one day." But nothing like that was up for sale.

He told me that I had to engage people, not wait for them to come to *me*. I had to make them want the book. "I'm telling you right now," he said, "I'm leaving here with a book today. I'm going to buy one of your books. It has something I need. I don't know what it is, but I know I need it. That's how you have to make these people feel." He pointed to the crowds roaming through the street.

I had a feeling this guy was lying to me, although he was very convincing in his monologue. But he never did buy a book from me, which is fair, because I didn't buy any of his stuff either.

I was going to debate this man's advice a bit when Christine called my name from behind me. She was sitting at our table on her phone. Her eyes were wide, and it looked like half her mouth wanted to laugh, but the other half didn't.

"Someone just stole your pen," she said. I peered down at the line of black, blue, green, and red pens that I laid next to a stack of books. I was now one black pen short. "Some lady walked up to the table," Christine continued, "and I thought she was going to say something to me, but she just grabbed one of the pens and slid it into her pocket and walked away."

At that, Christine started cracking up. She pointed in the direction the thief fled, and I looked up to see an elderly woman with windshield-caliber glasses looking back at me. She had a hand in her pocket and smirked when I made eye contact with her. I looked back at Christine, and I couldn't help but laugh, too. In the few hours of this event, there were only two people—three, if you counted Christine—who viewed me as a legitimate author, or even just a plain old writer. Even though I had dozens of books, a pile of articles about it, and stacks of bookmarks on my display table, few people seemed to understand that I was a writer selling his book, and instead viewed it exactly as it was titled: a junk sale.

One woman visited my booth to tell me that someone wanted to charge her six hundred dollars to remove a small nightstand from her apartment. "Can you believe it?" she shouted, her voice small and raspy. "*Six hundred dollars.* I told them they were crazy. They want too much money just to haul away some junk." She looked to be in her late sixties and was fair skinned and petite. She had a plain, royal blue flat-rimmed baseball cap askew on her head, and her backpack was strung over one shoulder as if she were late for algebra class at the senior center. "And *also,*" she told me, "*they* were the one's keeping the nightstand. So they were going to charge *me* so that *they* could take it away and probably sell it for a profit." She left my booth twice before coming back to say that she would look me up, and *maybe* she would buy my book online. "I don't have any cash on me now," she explained, and when I told her I accepted credit card, she scowled and wished me luck before departing my booth for the third and final time.

Another person approached me to tell me about how majestic yard sales can be. He was a small, stocky man who looked to be just short of his eightieth birthday. The skin on his arms and hands were pale, but his face had an olive tone to it, and I imagined that this man spent the entire summer outdoors while wearing a winter coat and mittens. "One man's junk is anotha's treasure," he proclaimed. "But the thing 'bout yard sales is ya ain't makin' a profit unless e'rything ya sell was given to ya. If ya sell things *you* bought, then ya gotta sell 'em for less than ya paid. Otherwise, ain't no one buyin' nothing." He looked at one of my displayed books and put his hand on the table. I stood in front of him, nodding and smiling. Then he added, "I'm glad someone else loves yard sales just as much as me."

Less than halfway through the event, I determined that most people probably didn't attend for the art and music; they were there to stroll down Main Street, grab some food, and see if anything caught their eye before dessert.

Other self-published authors who visited the event were particularly intrigued by my booth. One man charged my table after spotting my books from across the street. He was tall and lanky. His skin was a rigid shade of bronze, like a healthy redwood, while his hair was silky white. He told me about how he was forced to move from the United States to Guinea as a teen. "I was put out in the fields and in the dirt and the grass and made to work all day long." He spoke as if he were reciting a ghost story, slow with emphasis on every other verb.

"What kind of work did you do?" I asked.

"All day, every day I worked out in those fields," he replied, "because my parents brought me out there so I could work. And I wrote a book about it. I've published four books." He handed me a bright blue and red business card with his name in bold letters and his book titles right below. I took the card and stuck it in my pocket as he continued to talk about himself. "My first book became big. I was almost on Oprah Winfrey's show. You know her?" He didn't wait for me to answer. If he had, I would've said no. "Her team wanted me to be on the show. They really wanted me to talk about my life on Oprah's show. But once she read the derogatory language and racial slurs in my book, she didn't want anything to do with me. She didn't want me on the show." I nodded, and although I couldn't see my facial expression, I imagine it was as lifeless as this man's chances of being on *The Oprah Winfrey Show.*

He shrugged. "Everyone uses racial slurs."

I thought about just nodding and shooing him away, but I couldn't let that one slide. "I don't," I responded, my face not altering expression. He stared at me for a few moments, his brow furrowed, probably trying to determine for sure whether I was serious or just joking.

I suppose once he realized I was serious, he sighed and said, "Ah, good." He turned his head toward my books, giving them one last glance, and then he waved to me and walked away.

I looked down at the pens sitting on my table. I had hid them behind a tall stack of my books that no one within a hundred-mile radius was interested in perusing. Several hours had passed since I had arrived, and looking down at those pens—one fewer than I had just a couple hours before—I discovered that I only really learned one thing this entire day: People will steal from you. They'll steal from you right in front of you and then grin in your face. Maybe a bigger person—mentally *or* physically—would've fought for his pen back. He would've shouted, and the thief would have retrieved the pen from her pocket, handed it back, and dashed away. Or, if the thief resisted, a bigger man might have had no problem forcefully rescuing what was rightfully his.

I like to think that I'm a reasonable person, not a coward, although I suppose that's not for me to decide. I often broadcast that I pick my battles, but that mental vetting process is not very thorough or logical. I can yell at a malfunctioning TV remote as if it murdered my puppy, but I can't summon the nerve to apprehend a thief in broad daylight. I reasoned that I came prepared with nearly a dozen pens, so one being stolen isn't that big of a deal. It doesn't change the fact that I've been stolen from before, and I'll be stolen from again. The best course of action is to treat these events as isolated incidents and prepare for the next unexpected pilfering.

As a precautionary measure, I hid my surviving pens in a safer place. No one acknowledged the existence of my stack of books, and I determined that no one will acknowledge these pens behind it either. In fact, I reasoned that if someone *did* acknowledge a book from that stack, then they were welcome to abduct one of my writing utensils. It's the least I could do for them.

I learned from my days as a waiter that people love pens, and, more importantly, people love stealing them. Some nights

I would start my shift with eight pens and end the night with three. And, consequently, I would scurry back to the managers' office and steal more pens, which all would be stolen from me before the end of the next week. The circle of a pen's life would spin.

Perhaps this woman was from my serving days, and all those years of stealing and being stolen from weren't over; now she had returned to make sure I know my place, not as an aspiring author but rather as an insecure plebe or the gum under her shoe.

DOUGHNUTS
AND DAYDREAMS

Restaurant staff is unlikely to spit in your food. Just a few hours into their first shift, servers and cooks get used to meals being returned to the kitchen. So they're not too insulted by the time you show up and send back your pork chop because it's "too white."

Realistically, a person could send a dish back for a plethora of reasons, all of which a server has little interest in; servers just want your dining experience to be over. One of the only ways to truly aggravate the eatery's employees is to be rude, scream, shout, slap, insult, threaten, and/or incessantly complain to whomever is in charge. Even then, there is little chance that a server, cook, or manager is willing to risk losing their job by spitting in your wagyu filet mignon with a white asparagus tower on the side. Besides, that's probably not even satisfying retaliation.

When I served at a chain restaurant, the complaints were as plentiful as Auto-Tune in pop music. Oftentimes, guests ordered dessert after detesting their entire meals, all while hurling insults at my service, and I'd contemplate pouring a little Tabasco on their lava cake. At least that would make their dining experience consistent all the way through. But I never went that far.

I left the restaurant industry around nine years ago, yet I still get a kick out of watching all sorts of culinary programs on TV. As much as I love food, it's the drama that pulls me in. And there's one man who has insulted nearly every eatery he's visited. It makes me wonder if he's ever had an employee intentionally taint his food.

You'd recognize his accent the moment you heard it. A native of Scotland, he moved to England when he was young. His cadence is a blend of Scottish and Stratfordian, like the third prince in line for the crown in a Shakespearean play. Even if you don't know him, you've learned from him. If you've ever called someone a "doughnut" but don't know why, I'll give you the sole reason: Chef Gordon Ramsay.

Name a reality cooking show, and chances are he's been on it. He's notorious for his coveted ability to shout and provoke—and use vulgar language that'd make a pirate hide his sword. He curses so much on his reality show *Kitchen Nightmares* that it sounds like he's sending Morse code over cable television.

The decade-old program was revived last year, but I still flip on the old episodes regularly. Ramsay visits failing restaurants and attempts to get them back on the track to success. In the show, he covers everything from the cosmetic and food issues to the boiling emotional and relationship problems of the owners and staff. Some episodes are like *The Jerry Springer Show* set in a bistro. The screaming matches are unrivaled, except by Ramsay's own tirades.

I think I get a little too much enjoyment out of the way Ramsay slams every single restaurant he visits. He's almost always absolutely correct though, at least in my eyes. The sloppy dishes, the ugly décor, the filthy kitchen, the dysfunctional owners—Ramsay hits the nail (or the owner) on the head every single time. He pinpoints the weaknesses of a failing establishment; he attacks them without restraint, and then he squeezes the shit out of them. He's turned decaying, bug-infested, patron-less dives into chophouses with class. Whether or not many of those restaurants go on to become successful—or even last longer than a few more weeks—is an entirely other story. Nevertheless, Ramsay has left his imprint, and it's up to the owners and staff to continue to uphold the same quality and standards that the chef had seemingly instilled in them in the few days he spent there.

I watch the show too often, I've found. I have favorite episodes and regularly go back and watch them again and again. It's gotten to the point my family takes the remote away from me when they come to visit, because they know what I'm going to put on the TV.

Although most of the episodes follow that similar format, the show never ceases to captivate me, until the boredom sets in between the show's falling action and resolution. If Ramsay *didn't* scream at the top of his lungs in every episode—and if he didn't do it with his own British accent—I would've lost interest a long time ago. I've even started watching YouTube videos of Ramsay demonstrating mundane culinary techniques. I've watched a single video of him cutting an onion more times than I've tied my shoes in the past year. It's oddly inspirational and magical, almost like visiting Sea World. It makes me want to do something more with my life. So tomorrow I plan to enroll in culinary school.

Ramsay is incisive and uncompromising. His demeanor is intimidating to nearly everyone he meets. He knows all angles of the culinary world. He first inspects the menu, and *always* finds that it is either too long, dirty, has spelling mistakes, or is not an accurate representation of what the kitchen serves. God forbid the menu also has *photos of food* on it—he'd rather find mouse droppings in his teacup. Pictures on a menu is a clear indicator of a shit restaurant (the only exception being New Jersey diners).

Once Ramsay folds the menu closed, or conversely tears it to shreds, he inspects the dining room table itself. The most obvious of flaws seems to pass under the owners' noses unnoticed, but Ramsay attacks them like a mongoose on snakes. Even a crater in a wall cannot be hidden by an ornament without Ramsay peeling away the obstruction and breaking the hole wider just for the hell of it. Before his food arrives, he is liable to meander through the establishment to pick out all of its blemishes. He might even exercise in between tables if his wait is too long.

Once his food is plated and delivered, he goes to town—not in the way you would expect a normal diner would, however. First, he criticizes the dish's presentation. The portion could be enormous, or the entrée might look like cat food, or the plate could be covered in an unsightly amount of parsley, or grease might be dripping from the flatware at first poke. The potential shortcomings are endless.

Eggplant parmesan, pizza, fava beans, crayfish masquerading as lobster, and every other entrée known to man are all dissected by Ramsay, like a frog in a biology class. Ramsay tastes the food while searching its guts, in a manner that would be horrifying if a surgeon ever tried. Pizza, which any sane person would eat by hand, is stabbed with a fork and scraped with a knife by Gordon Ramsay. It's either doughy or undercooked, or just plain inedible because of the frozen or spoiled ingredients with which it was made. Soup is often greasy and flavorless; steaks are chewy and over seasoned; international dishes are void of any flare and zest.

"The chicken was frozen and reheated," Ramsay declares about his chicken masala. "Is anything here fresh?" When that question leaves his mouth, the viewer knows the answer, and so does Ramsay: no. The freezer and the microwave are the chefs in a failing kitchen, as they are in the households of many American families, too.

"Flush it down the toilet," Ramsay tells his server as he hands her his mutilated entrée. And she scurries back to the kitchen to relay the chef's recommendation to the back-of-house staff.

Ramsay already knows what's wrong with the kitchen just by tasting the food. He doesn't even have to visit the scullery itself to identify most issues. Years and years of culinary education and professional experience have made him as adept as your most renowned chefs. I, with no culinary education and very, *very* minimal restaurant experience, long to be as intuitive when I go out to eat.

After witnessing the disastrous places Ramsay has toured during his *Kitchen Nightmares* tenure, eating out has become less frequent for me than I otherwise would partake. On occasions when I do migrate out of my own kitchen, I often feel the urge to ask my server if I may see the back of house before I order, but I never satisfy that impulse. I resolve to inspect what is right in front of me, in the way Ramsay would right before he's about to curse out the restaurant's owners.

Most, if not all, of the restaurants I visit are far from fine dining and likely very successful. They are less inclined to care that one florescent bulb has burned out in the hallway by the bathrooms. If I told my server that there was a stain on my menu, he probably would laugh in my face, just as I might have done if someone said that same thing to me when I was in his shoes. If I left a Yelp review that condemned the distasteful Formica ledges of the host stand, I'd expect to become as detested as all of the other social media snitches who use their keyboards instead of just shutting up and moving on.

When I channel my inner Ramsay while out to eat, my mind goes berserk—*before* I've even had a chance to taste the kitchen's offspring. By the time my meal has arrived, I'm ready to mentally review it.

I've been fortunate enough to receive regular homemade and delicious meals growing up, and I enjoy cooking as much as the next Millennial father, but that doesn't mean I have any idea what I'm doing when I mince garlic or caramelize an onion. So when an entrée is placed in front of me at a restaurant, my critique of it is just as valuable as a sting ray's advice on how to build a treehouse. However, Ramsay has taught me, rather indirectly, that no restaurant can be perfect, and there *must* be something wrong with my entrée. I have no clue how most of the dishes I order are *supposed* to be presented, so I have to automatically assume that each restaurant does it incorrectly.

I cut a tiny sliver of the main course and chew it curiously. Truthfully, I enjoy nearly everything I order out, but every so often I'm delivered the insides of my baby's diaper. Oh, how I wish I too could persuade my server to taste a particularly dreadful meal. Ramsay casually demands it as if he *always* has had people taste his food, like royalty who's afraid of being poisoned by his staff.

Years of serving, however, have conditioned me much more

than hours and hours of *Kitchen Nightmares* have, and I'm only inclined to return a dish if it is overwhelmingly inedible, or incorrect altogether. Oftentimes, I simply pick at the edible pieces of the meal and pray dessert is better.

THE MONEY PIT
IN THE 'BURBS

As an elementary school kid, still tracing the alphabet on the drab pages of a glossy-covered workbook, I was under the impression that I was to move out of my parents' house the day I turned eighteen. Or perhaps the day later, after I'd had plenty of birthday cake and ice cream. My parents didn't tell me that, but even at six I knew that being eighteen years old made you an adult, and adults don't live with their parents. In fact, by the fifth grade, I was pretty confident that my father was already anticipating my departure. Some evenings when he got home from work, he would look at me with a "What are you still doing here?" glare, the kind your roommate gives you when he brings a girl back to the dorm. Then my father would smirk and proclaim in his booming voice, "Hi, Dad, nice to see you! How was work?"

I would return, "Great, son! Thanks for asking."

He was hinting that he wanted me to greet him first, before he had to acknowledge me, sitting on his couch, watching his TV, eating his dark chocolate, which I didn't even care for, frankly. But he expected too much, because the afterschool special was *Zoboomafoo*. I pretended I was too old for that show, but no male really is too old to enjoy the hijinks of monkeys, fictional or not.

Being spiteful, a trait which I'm convinced will be my fatal flaw, I never greeted him first. Every day, I waited for my father to say, "Hi, Dad, nice to see you! How was work?" And I would deliver the same response again and again. It was a charming back and forth, save for the fact that I was the only one who got a kick out of it.

I did it once when my dad's parents were visiting. I had returned home from school earlier that afternoon and spent the later part of the day sitting in the living room with them. My grandfather, a World War II veteran, was absorbed in The History Channel, tsk-ing whenever Adolf Hitler's name was mentioned. My grandmother was less interested, especially when she had a Jude Deveraux novel in hand. I sat next to my grandfather on the couch in front of the TV. I wasn't familiar with the lingo the narrator used when describing the Battle of Normandy—terms like liberation, belligerents, and sectors—but when the narrator mentioned "amphibious assault," I took a moment to point out, "You know, PopPop, a newt is actually an amphibian. Salamanders, too."

"That's great, Patrick," he said, without looking away from the TV.

When my father returned home that evening and stomped past the living room, he greeted me the same way he had done the three dozen evenings prior. "Hi, Dad, nice to see you! How was work?"

This time, I imagine my grandpa was confused, thinking my dad was talking to him. Yet, my grandpa hadn't worked that day or any day since he retired more than a decade earlier. If my grandpa intended to reply, I beat him to it with my usual response.

PopPop then turned to me and laughed so jovially that he accidentally swatted the remote off the couch. My father was already around the corner at this point, but after he heard his dad laugh, he laughed too, bellowing throughout the house. It caused my mother to peek her head in from the backyard, where she had been sunbathing, and ask what Dad was laughing about.

That's a good sign, I thought, and figured maybe I wouldn't have to move out anytime soon.

I lasted another fifteen years in my parents' home, never forced to vacate due to being a chronic pain in the ass. By our mid-twenties, Christine and I talked about living together, maybe even buying a place. At the time, the market was still reasonable, so we quickly began our search.

After months of looking for a house within our budget, Christine and I put an offer on a home surrounded mostly by farmland. It was the only single-family home we had seen within our budget. We had looked at the house twice before, and we were sure we kind of liked it. So our realtor recommended a mortgage lender, who got us set up for preapproval. It's a process akin to being hazed before being inducted into a fraternity.

I had done my best to save money and build my credit score over the years, but it doesn't count for anything; no matter how good your credit score is, finance people will casually snicker in your face if you try to defend it. You need to have great credit for roughly, I'd say, four centuries before it makes a difference. George Washington still wouldn't be able to get a decent rate on a colonial in Vermont. He'd be told to try again in 2150.

Christine and I were prodded by the mortgage broker for what felt like six hours but very well could have been about twelve minutes. "How much do you have saved?" he asked. "Where do you work? What's the address? What kind of work is it? *Exactly* how much do you make annually?"

"Gross or net?" I replied.

"Gross."

"I actually don't know what any of this means. I was just trying to sound smart."

The mortgage broker was happy to answer all of our questions, even mundane ones like, "Can we afford this house?"

We received our preapproval over the phone and submitted

our offer that afternoon. A day and a half later, after a counter-offer from the seller and a counter-counteroffer from us, we were one step closer to owning a cape cod in New Jersey.

The home was in a rural town in one of the most rural counties in the state. The probability of getting stuck behind a tractor during your commute was about as high as the probability of seeing a taxicab in New York City.

The house had two bedrooms on the second floor, each about the size of four ping pong tables pressed together, and a half-bath that was just a walk-in closet with plumbing. On the first floor was a large full bathroom with a Jacuzzi and separate shower. There also was a carpeted eat-in kitchen as well as a hardwood-floored bistro area that couldn't comfortably fit a nightstand and a folding chair. I figured this was where I could stack piles of the books I've purchased over the years, floor to ceiling, as if I were bricking it closed off to the world like Montresor did to his friend in "The Cask of Amontillado."

The yard was a quarter acre, mostly taken up by the hump of a massive septic tank partially buried underground. On the side of the hump that faced the back of the house, the seller had built a wall with shale. The rest of the hump was covered in grass. It resembled a stage, one nymphs might use to put on Shakespearean plays. I was excited to use it as a stage for friends in indie bands. Spring was nearing, which meant that the perfect time for outdoor shows wasn't far away. There were only two houses nearby, one on either side of ours. The larger had been vacant for several years and was likely going to be razed

soon. The other was slightly smaller than the one we were buying, recently purchased by a guy our age. I figured he wouldn't
mind punk and bluesy rock cleaving the thick country air late
into the night. Worst case scenario, maybe the sometimes-
somber, sometimes-chaotic melodies blistering Peavey amps
would be enough to send him into a comfortable slumber.

The shows will go on, I thought, *because this is* my *house.*

The next night, our mortgage broker sent us our pre-
approved interest rate. It was double what we expected. When
I called him to discuss, all he offered was a cheap sigh before
saying, "Look, it can turn out to be lower than that. Or it could
wind up being a little bit higher. You just don't qualify for a
rate much lower than what I've given you."

"But I wanted to host concerts."

I ran the numbers several times with Christine, something
our mortgage broker never bothered to do with us. We calculated time after time that our monthly mortgage payments
would be about as much as we were taking home a month,
which left little room for the cost of utilities, groceries, gas, and
the more-than-occasional Shake Shack run. Christine and I
had no choice but to back out. Our lawyer canceled the contract
while in attorney review, and we were back to house hunting.

We didn't find another home we liked within our budget for a
whole year. If the cost wasn't a concern with a place, more often
than not it was a fixer upper. Most homes in our price range
needed to be demolished and rebuilt. One we previewed had

such a strong black mold presence that an abandoned couch in the front room looked as though it were wearing the blotches of a Rorschach test. Another home had a variety of colorful electrical wires hanging from the ceiling that looked like vines in the amazon.

When a home wasn't a fixer upper, it was small enough that it could fit into the trunk of a Chevy Tahoe. Part of our problem was that we were looking for a home in one of the most expensive states in the country. The other problem was that Christine and I were (and still are) in so much student-loan debt. Now, I'm not so unwitting that I don't take responsibility for my own loan dues. I knew exactly what I was doing when I signed those papers. If I wanted to go to college—which I did—I was to take out massive loans with high interest rates, or take one class a semester at a community college for the next nineteen years. I thought the same way every eighteen-year-old does right after he graduates from high school: *Give me about six years and I'll be a millionaire.*

I had no idea how I would make even a few thousand dollars, let alone a million, but that mentality only helped to diminish the gravity of the loans I was taking out every year. I wasn't totally oblivious to what I was doing, though. I calculated how much money room and board would cost me for four years at school, and I nixed it the moment I hit the equal tab on my calculator.

Although I had been paying back my student loans since freshman year of college, I was still deep into it, and Christine and I separately were making what felt like rent payments toward our loans. Even still, I wasn't sure whether I had made the right or wrong decision in taking this route. Student loan debt is so complicated that even after years of torment you don't know if you're headed up the ladder of success or down a narrow spiral staircase to further anguish, agony, and despair. It's like a toxic relationship, but you're too poor to break up.

The second home for which we submitted an offer was in a town we didn't particularly like. We were used to the country-side homes in the central and northwestern parts of the state, no matter how beat up they might be. This house, though, was farther south, sat directly at the exit of a major highway, and had a Popeyes on the corner of the street. It was a much larger home and had a larger lot as well. It was newly updated, which is realtor talk for "Shitty Flip," but our agent didn't seem to be concerned about that, so neither were we. It didn't have a great smell—soggy polyester doused in bug spray—but I blamed the new construction, hoping it'd dissipate after a few weeks.

The house also was owned by a bank, another red flag that didn't seem to worry our agent, who had only been in the business a year and was used to selling homes in one of the wealthiest counties in the state—not within fifty miles of where we were looking. She had worked with us to find a home within our budget, but we needed to expand our search. Every few weeks that we didn't find a home, Christine and I added a new town to our list.

"How about Fieldsboro?" I'd say to Christine.

"Where even is that?" she'd reply.

"Somewhere, I think. I'll add it to the list."

When attorney review was dragging, our agent warned us that someone could sweep in and give a better offer to steal the house from us. She bugged me twice a day to follow up with our attorney.

"Just think," she told us, "how would you feel if you lost the house tomorrow?"

After nearly a year and a half of searching, I wasn't interested in losing another home, even if I hated the area and thought the house smelled bad.

After attorney review concluded, without anyone else trying to steal the house out from under us, we were authorized to schedule the inspection of the home and property. Christine and I were present with our realtor during the inspection, which took a couple hours. A thin man with glasses and wiry gray hair walked up the driveway as we waited inside our parked car. He wore an expensive black Canon with a wide-angle lens around his neck, a sharp contrast to his lacteous skin.

He took dozens of photos of the exterior and interior of the house. We watched him squeeze himself into every crawl space and climb up the master closet into the attic. He even shimmied himself underneath the deck, somehow without a flashlight.

When he was done, he met with us in the kitchen and said, "There are two major problems that I can recall without reviewing my notes. First, the water heater is leaking. Doesn't work." He looked at the three of us, as if waiting for a response, but we just nodded. "Second, this house is on a dual heat system." He said it almost like a question. "Well, the upstairs is broke. Can't say how much it'll cost to fix. Could be a lot. Could be a little." He turned off the camera around his neck by twisting a nob on the top. "But otherwise the house is pretty okay."

It was almost as if he knew exactly what we were looking for: a house that was pretty okay.

The house wasn't pretty okay, however. Aside from the water heater and heating system, it had some monumental issues. I suppose it was structurally sound, but the house was a money pit, something we promised ourselves we wouldn't invest in.

Almost every windowsill was rotted; there was termite damage in a crawl space, moss growing all over the roof, cracks and structural damage to the chimney, black mold in the laundry room, electrical outlets that didn't work or were wired incorrectly, and a slimy slew of other concerns. We made a list of thirty-two issues that needed to be remedied, the most superficial of which was a busted window in the crawl space that was being fed by a rusted gutter downspout, resulting in even more water damage to an already questionable home.

When we told our realtor we wanted out, she didn't understand why we wouldn't just send our demands to the seller, to the *bank*, a heartless, faceless entity that wouldn't lose any sleep if the house caved in on us the night after closing.

"I can deal with a lot of these issues," I told our agent one afternoon over the phone. "But we don't have the money to pay for most of them. For example, if the chimney needs to be replaced, that would cost more than the down payment we're putting on the house right now."

"I understand," she said. "But just remember how much you and Christine loved the house when you first saw it."

She was right, indicating that we had loved the house when we first saw it. The master bedroom, which took up the entire second floor, had its own recently renovated bathroom, and it also had two large closets, one and a half for Christine and half for me. But when I thought beyond that, there really wasn't much else I cared for. It's like having a crush on someone in middle school. Your hormones are so out of whack that you're attracted to a different person every week. At some point you consider obsessing over people in alphabetical order so that every girl gets a chance.

Our agent ended our call by saying, "Let me know what you decide." But I never did let her know what Christine and I decided. After I hung up with our agent, I called our lawyer and told him we wanted out, and he sent a letter detailing such that afternoon. Neither Christine nor I spoke to our agent again.

Four months later, we reconnected with one of the first real estate agents with whom we had worked, named Harry. He had shown us some houses and condos in the beginning of our search, but then we lost touch after a few months of finding nothing. Compared to the rest, Harry had far superior knowledge and experience. It felt like trading up a Fisher-Price toy drill for a DeWalt twenty volt.

We found a house we liked within two weeks of working with Harry. New roof, waterproofed basement with a new water heater and sump pump, new breezeway between the house and two-car garage. Not only was this the first house we had looked at with a garage—let alone a *two*-car garage—but the word "new" was peppered all around the listing like coworkers around a tray of cookies.

The house was equidistant between my job and Christine's, and it was in a town with which we were familiar. That same evening, we submitted an offer, along with six other people, we later found out. Four people bid higher than we did, and we lost the house before we could even imagine ourselves living in it.

During the next three months, the same trend followed, and there seemingly was no home on which we could bid high enough. We just kept getting beat out by other couples. I didn't know if money was our problem or just not enough heart, like an athlete who remains unsigned throughout an entire offseason.

At the end of the summer, though, we found a house worth competing for. It was old and small—not Chevy Tahoe-trunk small, but unpretentious nonetheless. It had enough room for the two of us and all the junk we've accrued throughout the years. But the home's main selling point was that it needed minimal work done.

This was a seventy-year-old with tons of plastic surgery. It was another cape cod, much like the first house on which we had put an offer. However, this one was heavily paneled. Much of the first floor, some of the second floor, and even every door in the house was paneled. I wondered if this had been a style years ago, or if the original owners were trying to confuse guests. "Why do you have so many doorknobs sticking out of your walls? And where do you pee?"

I figured it was easy enough to swap out doors. And lumber's cheap, right? (It's not.) I didn't spend much time worrying about it. In the dining room, there was a monstrous china cabinet built into the wall. It had enough storage space to hide all of Willy Wonka's Oompa Loompas, or at least all the ones who appeared in the original movie. The china cabinet also was covered in hideous dark paneling. It brought down the incandescence of the room several hundred lumens. *Oh well*, I thought, *paint's cheap too, right?* (Also not.)

Nearly all of the appliances were decades old. In appliance-years, that's like finding a person who was alive during the American Civil War. Each room also needed to be repainted. It was dark and raining the first two times we looked at the house, and the current paint scheme wasn't doing the interior any favors. I felt like I was back in a middle school science lab during a lockdown drill, except that I didn't have anyone coughing directly into my ear canal.

The basement at one time had been completely finished. The dark paneling and baseboard heaters remained intact on the walls, but whatever flooring there once was had been removed, leaving just the bare cement floor and scrawls of glue stains. In the back corner of the basement were Bilco doors that led out to the backyard. I took note of how dry the basement was. It looked like *maybe* there were some water stains, but the cement was dry by the doors, even though it had rained nonstop for the past couple days. I took that as a good sign.

Christine's childhood home flooded several times while she was growing up, so one of our biggest concerns was finding a home outside of a flood zone. If a house was even near a FEMA-sanctioned flood zone, we ruled it out.

After previewing the house twice, Christine and I submitted an offer. A month went by before we heard anything concrete. The owners were likely waiting for a better offer, or if they had already received a better offer, they were waiting for a better offer than that one. I understood, but after two years of house hunting, I didn't keep my spirits high. We continued to look for other homes and apartments with reasonable rent, but there was nothing. Anything that remotely interested us was listed for sale and then in "pending" status before we could even schedule a day to visit.

Supposedly, more people are moving out of New Jersey annually than any other state in the country—a stat every true New Jerseyan cherishes—but when you're buying a home, it feels like the opposite.

Finally, at the beginning of the following month, the owners countered our offer. We agreed, and so attorney review began for us once again.

From attorney review to inspection to appraisal to closing—it took a month and a half. About sixteen times during the course of those six or so weeks, I thought for sure the deal would fall through, and then we'd once again be on the endless, forlorn trail of house hunting. By the time we closed, midway through the fall, I didn't really care what happened. I mean, I cared, but I had conditioned myself to not care in the event we lost the house.

After closing, the very first thing I did to the house was rip out all the floor molding. I just hated it for some reason, even though I barely noticed it. We didn't begin any serious work on the house, however, until day two. My parents came over, donning blemished denim, and we cleaned. The house had a persistent odor somewhere between wet gym socks and a mesquite-flavored beef stew. It wasn't pleasant, even while wearing a surgical mask.

That same day, one day after closing, we noticed water by the Bilco basement doors. What I learned was that after two days of rain, our basement retains water, which means that in the event of a biblical-level flood, our basement wouldn't make it through the first morning. We resolved to keep an inflatable raft down there in case things went south.

When my mom ran the washing machine to clean it out, the pipe backed up, and water spilled all around the washer and dryer. Christine's plumber friend came out four days later to take a look. After about an hour of examining the washer and pipes, he figured there might be a minor clog in the exit sewer pipe toward the front of our house. He had me run some water and flush the toilet twice while he looked at the pipes near the washer.

After the second flush, I heard a crashing wave in the front of our basement. I ran down the stairs, expecting to see a burst pipe pouring water everywhere. All I saw was discolored water slowly expanding throughout the front corner of the basement. It was a grotesque slime monster out of a 1960s science-fiction film. In the center, a hole was bubbling. The cap that was previously covering the hole had popped off, and shredded, soaked fragments of toilet paper and fecal matter were circled around it. The odor I was so determined to get rid of was now sufficiently masked by the odor of what came pouring out of this pipe.

Christine came running down the basement steps behind me, and then our friend walked into frame from the back corner of the basement. "Yeah," he said, "that's not good."

Our system had backed up, because it had been clogged, he told us, likely before we even bought the house. I wondered how many different people's poop was sitting on our basement floor, and why did they use so much toilet paper?

Our friend recommended some cleanup crews and plumbers who could snake and scope out the pipe for us, as he didn't bring that equipment with him and didn't live or work close enough to return soon.

After a few more minutes of us soaking in our own somberness, he left, and I just kept staring at that pile of toilet paper and shit. It was about the size of a papier-mâché volcano that fourth-grade students make. The eruption was a lot larger, though. It covered about fifteen-square-feet. I've never seen a papier-mâché volcano do that. I imagined how an elementary school teacher might react if toilet paper and shit started spewing out of a students' homemade volcano, and I bit down on my lower lip to fight back a snicker. Then I looked at the sewage on my basement floor and instantly frowned.

"You want me to call the cleanup crew?" Christine asked me. "I don't know how much it'll cost."

"No," I said, grabbing a broom and dustpan from the rack on the far wall. "I'll take care of it."

"Is there anything I can do?"

"Can you grab me a garbage bag, please? The bigger the better."

As Christine ran up the stairs into the kitchen, I began sweeping the crap and toilet paper into the dustpan, which would be tossed into the garbage along with the rest of this mess. I tried to keep thinking positively, reminding myself that I was a homeowner. But when I said it now, it sounded much more like a taunt than an encouraging affirmation.

2B OR NOT 2B

I celebrated becoming a homeowner by sweeping up human feces from my basement floor. The sewer backed up several days after closing on the house. Fecal matter and soaked balls of toilet paper lay on the floor in hills, like papier-mâché volcanoes at a fourth-grade science fair. Between home and work, where a coworker dropped a turd outside my office, I couldn't seem to get away from shit. Maybe I had missed my calling as a plumber or manure manufacturer.

Christine and I had not yet moved into the house. We had been there every day since closing to clean, repair, and find out what else wasn't working. It started simple, with doors that wouldn't close. Bedroom, bathroom, and closet doors would stick against the doorjamb and stop about a half inch or so from shutting all the way, as if the doors were too wide for the frame. You could slam them as hard as you'd like, but the best that would do was get them stuck, which, as it turned out, was just as frustrating as the doors not closing at all.

Our problems eventually graduated to technological challenges: outlets wired incorrectly, flickering lights, an inoperable dishwasher—which worked perfectly during inspection—and an oven that smoked whenever its temperature rose above two hundred degrees Fahrenheit. The house was structurally sound, meaning that the structure made a lot of sounds. On several occasions—before we even moved in—Christine thought she heard someone breaking into the house. I thought maybe it was the house settling, even though it already had nearly seventy years to settle. *Maybe we just bought a home with commitment issues*, I thought. The noises she was hearing, however, were from the clogged gutters and baseboard radiators. In an empty house, those two instruments harmonize as well as whales and car alarms, creating what sounds like a clumsy burglar fumbling through a living room window.

Each hour we spent at the house, we found something new that needed either to be fixed or professionally eradicated. Our most pressing issue became the sewage backup. The night it happened, neither Christine nor I dared to flush another toilet. After we cleaned up the mess, we drove to her mother's home, where we were living, bladders full. We stayed away from our newly purchased property for a couple days afterward.

During that time, the only thing I could think to do was make a list of what needed to be done. It was long and overwhelming, and I was convinced Mars would be colonized before we could cross all of the chores off the list. So, separately, I made myself a three-step list. Identifying the issues with the house was the first step; learning how to fix them was the second step; applying those methods and actually fixing the problems was the third step.

Step one for the backup was completed shortly after shit, toilet paper, and sewer water erupted all over the basement floor. We didn't need a professional to tell us that shouldn't happen. We hoped it was a clog and not a burst pipe or something more serious, but we wouldn't know until we had a plumber thoroughly examine the system below our basement.

Step two was to call a plumber to snake out the pipe first, then scope it with a camera. We tried contacting local plumbers but didn't get ahold of anyone.

During the pandemic, more people than usual were working from home, schooling from home, and just staying inside in general, which meant frequent sewer problems and major business for plumbers. As a result, those we tried calling in the surrounding area were so busy that they couldn't even answer their phones.

We eventually found a commercial plumber that had a location just a town over. They are a nationally recognized plumbing and water cleanup company, mostly known for a catchy jingle they used to run on television commercials. Without much optimism, Christine gave them a call and got someone on the first ring. They had a plumber ready to go for us and sent him out later that same afternoon.

A large, lanky man with pale skin and a square head pulled up our driveway in a white kidnapper's van. I've never met someone who drives a van like that, but it's possible they serve some purpose other than luring children with promises of candy and puppies. The man exited the van, somehow already smiling, and greeted in a deep Eastern European accent, "Pat and Christine? Pawl, the plumber. I hear you had a backup. Show me the way." He extended his hand outward, and I thought he was looking for a low-five. I raised my hand to about the height of my chest to slap it down, until I realized he was gesturing for us to guide him to the basement.

We led Pawl to our backyard and through the Bilco doors into our basement. Near the base of the steps below the doors was a large, vertical cast iron pipe that funnels all of our shower, sink, and toilet water into the pipes underground and out to the township sewer line. This caught his eye first. He scratched his scruffy chin and nodded. Then he turned around and said, "All right, show me what the problem is."

I pointed to the front of the basement, only about twenty feet from this cast iron pipe. On the ground were two caps that covered the exit pipe under the cement floor. The one on the left would guide you in the direction of the cast iron pipe, and the one on the right would lead you out through the front yard and into the street. The right cap was the one that had exploded two nights before and enabled our basement to succumb to a foul bath. After cleaning everything up, I didn't press the cap back onto the pipe and instead placed it on an angle on top so that it wouldn't get stuck. Pawl lifted the cap with his bare hand and tossed it to the side. He gazed into the hole where the pipe sat. The water was still resting close to the top of the pipe. Pawl chuckled and stood up to look at Christine and me.

He seemed to tower over us. In fairness, Christine and I are short, so most people seem to tower over us. But in this instance I felt like a third grader in the principal's office.

"Yup, it's clogged," Pawl said. "Probably a lot of toilet paper or something else that shouldn't be flushed." He looked at Christine. "Flush any wipes or cleaning products? Pads? Anything like that?" He didn't wait for her to answer, but she still said "No" over his booming voice. "That's a big no-no. Let me get my snake, and we'll get this taken care of." Then Pawl blew past us and ran out to his van.

Pawl returned to the basement a few minutes later, lugging what looked like a mini sit-on lawnmower without the cushioned seat. It was about the size of the luggage you'd use if you were moving out of your home for good. It looked to weigh about the same. Pawl was out of breath by the time he dropped it next to the exit pipe hole. Christine had gone upstairs to work a few minutes earlier, leaving just me and the plumber in the basement now. He was humming an upbeat tune as he untangled the contraption's wires, but his naturally low voice offset the melody to make it sound unsettling. I love horror films, and I now felt like I was living one. I wondered what Pawl might use to murder me.

Rolled up neatly on the side of the machine was the snake, which went into the drain. Maybe he planned to use that to strangle me, I thought. Or maybe the machine had a secret compartment that hid his knives and nunchucks. Or maybe it shot poison darts!

Pawl pulled the power cable from the back of the machine and handed it to me. *Oh no,* I thought, *does he want me to wrap this around my own neck?*

"Can you plug this in for me?" he asked.

I exhaled, relieved, and took the cable from him, plugging it into the nearest outlet. Pawl continued humming, and to the melody of his song, he sang, "And *here* we *go!*" Pawl reached down and hit the power button. A little light at the top of the machine turned red. "Huh." He clapped his hands once. Then he reached down and hit the power button two more times. The little red light flickered. "I don't think there's enough power. Is there another outlet you can plug this into?" I tried a second outlet, and the same thing happened.

Pawl stopped humming and kicked the machine with his heal, cursing as he did it. I tried a third outlet, and when the red light illuminated again, Pawl kicked the machine two more times, nearly knocking it over. On the fourth try, the machine did the same thing, and so did Pawl, only cursing louder this time. It was an abusive step dance of some sort. I had the urge to breakdance next to him to lighten the tension, but I was afraid of pulling a muscle, which I suppose would've served its purpose.

In the midst of kicking his motorized drain snake, Pawl must've had an idea. He suddenly stopped and ran out to his truck without saying a word to me. He came back with a bright orange extension cord, plugged its female end into the snake's power cable, and handed the male end to me.

"Can you plug this in somewhere upstairs maybe?" he asked. His voice was still deep, but it was quieter now.

I took the extension cord from him and ran it to a kitchen outlet. When Pawl flicked the power switch on and the little red bulb lit up again, I thought for sure I'd be murdered. I was standing on the basement steps, watching Pawl, not the machine. I was prepared for him to lift his leg to kick it again, but he took a step toward it instead and got on one knee, as if he were about to propose to it.

"I think I know what to do," he said. "Just give me about ten minutes."

I went upstairs to wait with Christine. She was sitting at a folding table, which acted as our dinner table, hiding behind her work laptop. I sat down across from her and said, "Remind me to tell you about how nuts this guy is."

"I can hear him clearly," she responded without taking her eyes off her computer screen.

A few minutes later, Pawl called me back into the basement. I'm not sure what he had done to the machine, but he had unplugged it from the extension cord and plugged it into a nearby outlet in the basement. He flipped the switch on, and a separate bulb illuminated lime green. The machine rumbled. "Now we're in business."

He started to unravel the snake line and shoved it down into the clogged pipe. It hit the bottom and cut right, following the pipe under the ground below our front yard. Once it was a few feet underground, Pawl hit a big black button on the side of his machine, which at this point must've been suffering from PTSD. The machine revved louder and started pushing the snake line out. Pawl explained that it was traveling the length of the sewer line and would push whatever is in there out to the township's sewer. As long as it was just a simple clog, it would solve our problem.

The snake ran out about sixty feet before Pawl hit a red button to stop it. Then he pressed a black button with an arrow on it, which made the snake pull back. When the snake returned, wrapped in a loop on the side of the machine, Pawl reached down to the ground. "Uh oh, this is not good," he said, shaking his head. "Look at this." He extended his hands toward me to show two thin roots. They looked like brown spaghetti, but frayed and dripping wet. Pawl tossed them into the corner of our basement. "This tells me you have a much bigger problem than a clogged sewer line. I'm going to give you some advice, and I really hope you think about this: you really need a sewer scope. I can do it right now. Even if you don't want it right now—if you don't want to go with me or my company— you should have this done sooner than later. It'll save you a lot of headache. I can do it right now, it you want. We'll be able to see exactly what the problem is and fix it."

"That's part of the reason we called you," I said. "Please do the scope today."

Pawl nodded and picked up his drain snake. He carried it back to his truck and returned a few minutes later with a machine equally as large, except this one had a little monitor attached to it. Pawl plugged it into a nearby outlet and hit the power button. It started up on the first try. If it hadn't, I was sure Pawl would kick the monitor part first, even in front of Christine, who had just joined us in the basement.

This machine was similar to the drain snake in that it also had a line that would travel through the pipes. This line's exterior was rubber, however—as opposed to wire—and had a small waterproof camera at the very end. It could've been something you'd use to inspect an elephant's rectum for all I knew. When Pawl jokingly pointed the camera at his face, his giant, square head was shown on the monitor attached to the machine.

Pawl dropped his scope into the left pipe, which led to the back of our basement, and he began to unreel it. As he did so, I took out my cellphone.

"Oh, good idea," Pawl said. "I was going to suggest you record this for yourself."

Truthfully, I didn't even consider recording the monitor. I just was checking the time. But at Pawl's tardy suggestion, I opened the camera app and began recording the sewer scope. Immediately, Pawl criticized our pipes. He stopped the camera when it came up to the point underneath the large cast iron pipe.

"This has been a problem for a very long time," he told us. "Basically what you're seeing now is the grease." But I didn't know *what* I was seeing. It looked like those medical renderings of a person's organs after fifty years of smoking cigarettes. I could see some white and red and gray, but these blobs of color were nothing more concrete to me than static on a television screen. The only detail I could make out clearly was the quarter-inch of water that sat at the base of the pipe. Still, I nodded, as if I knew exactly what he was talking about.

Pawl slowly pulled the camera back, and it traveled in reverse through the pipe. He stopped it right underneath us. "See how the pipe's channeled, looks like Christmas?" he asked. I didn't see Christmas. I saw a smoker's anus. He didn't wait for me to answer and said, "Shouldn't look like that." He further explained that that's a major problem, and the entirety of the pipes from this point to the large pipe needed to be replaced. He then pulled out the camera and dropped it into the next hole, which led out to the street.

Pawl slowly pushed the camera through the sewer line, which looked identical to the last one. "See how it's channeled?" he said of this sewer line. "Your pipe basically is running in dirt. The bottom of the pipe has pretty much worn out." He sighed, as if sad for us. The sewer line declined in depth, and Pawl indicated that this drop signified that those pipes belonged to the township. "See how the pipe changes from your ugly one to a pretty one?" He pulled the camera back and forth a couple times to show the change in pipes.

It wasn't obvious to me. It was the difference between Dutch chocolate ice cream and regular chocolate ice cream. The dissimilarities were subtle, but I couldn't tell you what was different.

"You guys are going to back up in no time," Pawl warned us, pulling the camera back in reverse. "This is just . . . This is just really bad." He stopped the camera midway through its return trip. "Look. There are the roots."

"I don't see them," I said. And I really didn't see them. I saw some clumps of familiar colors, but I couldn't identify any cracks. I didn't see any dirt, and I did not see any roots.

"They're right there," Pawl said, but he continued to pull back the camera as he spoke. "This is really bad. This is not good."

I hit the stop button on my phone and shoved the phone into my pocket.

"We have to replace *all* of the pipes," Pawl told us. "You can't keep these old ones. They're all finished."

"How much is this going to cost us?" Christine asked.

"I'm going to have to make a call. I'll get you a really good deal. You guys are in a great spot as new homeowners." I didn't know what any of this gibberish meant. I just wanted to know how much it would cost, and obviously Christine did, too.

"I just have to make a call," Pawl repeated. "Give me about fifteen minutes. I'll be right back." Then Pawl picked up the sewer scope and lugged it back out to his van.

Pawl returned about twenty minutes later with a clipboard. First, he wanted us to pay him for his services. He broke down the itemized receipt: costs of the snake, the scope, and the labor. Christine wrote him a check, and he shoved it into his pocket. Underneath that paperwork was another sheet of paper with an estimate for replacing all of our pipes. Pawl pulled the clipboard away from us and pressed it against his chest.

"Now look," he said. "Let me explain to you what needs to be done." He walked us over to the large cast iron pipe that ran vertically against the back wall of our basement. "This needs to be changed. This can't stay. This should've been replaced ages ago. Then what we're going to do is jackhammer back here—we get all the permits." He pointed to the base of the cast iron pipe and swung his arm all the way to the front of the basement. "All along here—all of these pipes need to be replaced. Then, we're going to replace the sewer line out in your front yard and all the way up to the street. We don't even dig up the yard. We get all the permits. We make all the arrangements. We have all of this covered. Once we're done, we put fresh cement down in your basement, and we're on our way. It's a really quick process. The longest part is waiting for the cement to dry."

Pawl took a breath and looked down at his clipboard. "Now, I made a call for you. I know you guys are new homeowners, so I wanted to get you a good deal. You guys won't be able to read my chicken scratch on the estimate, so I'll just break it down for you. My boss knocked two thousand dollars off the total." I held my breath. When you get a two-thousand-dollar discount on *anything*, you're still overpaying. "This is a really great deal. I wouldn't wait, because you have a huge problem."

He showed us the estimate on his clipboard. "It's going to cost eighteen thousand dollars. That's for parts, labor, pulling permits—the whole nine yards." With taxes and fees, that came out to a total of nineteen thousand four hundred eighty-four dollars and twenty-six cents. That was a brand new Nissan Sentra.

We took the clipboard from Pawl and stared at it for what felt like several minutes.

"Listen," he said, "you guys are in a really good spot, being new homeowners. This can be taken care of right away, and then you don't have to worry about it for the rest of your lives. My company offers an eighteen-month interest-free financing option. I'd call about that right away. I wouldn't wait. You're going to have another backup real soon."

When neither Christine nor I spoke, Pawl continued. "You don't have to make a decision now. Take a day or two. But don't wait too long. In the meantime, do *not* use the toilet. Number ones might be okay for a few days, maybe weeks. But if you have to do number two, go down the road to the Wawa or CVS. Do not flush anything other than liquids down the toilet."

Pawl took the clipboard back and handed us the estimate. We walked him out to his van through the Bilco doors, while he reminded us not to wait too long to call him to get our sewer line replaced. He handed me his business card, hopped into his van, and took off down the road.

Christine made the executive decision to call our realtor, Harry, to weigh our options. We tried reaching out to our attorney first, but he obviously wanted nothing to do with us. We closed on the house; he made his commission. Nothing else here would make him money and instead would solely be a waste of his time and energy.

When we tried Harry, he suggested suing everyone, including himself.

"That's just the way it is," he said, with no inflection in his voice to suggest he was being facetious. Neither Christine nor I liked the idea of suing *anyone*, let alone the people who helped us buy our first home. But if that was going to save us from ultimately losing our house, that's what had to be done.

Harry advised us to get a second opinion first. He told us that in his several decades in real estate, the plumbing company we had just used had the worst track record of any business he has dealt with. Their competition were basically Olympic sprinters, and this company was the guy limping in the back with a Glock, taking out the knees of the runners ahead of him one by one.

One of Harry's recent clients had this company come out to her house for the same exact issue we had. They snaked her drain no problem, but then during the sewer scope, they told her it was absolutely vital that she replace her sewer line as soon as possible; otherwise, the entire system would implode, something pipes are not typically known to do on short notice. They told her it would cost twenty thousand dollars and gave her the same disconcerting spiel Pawl gave Christine and me. The woman called a second one of their local offices to come take a look at her pipes, and they told her the same thing. Harry recommended that she reach out to a plumber from Trenton who was a trusted tradesman for many of Harry's clients over the years. The Trenton plumber came out, scoped her pipes, and found only one minor issue that cost her a couple hundred dollars to fix.

"It's been more than a year," Harry said, "and she hasn't had any plumbing problems since."

Harry gave us the name of the business: O'Lawlor Plumbing & Heating. We got in touch with the owner, Francis O'Lawlor, the next day and had him come out immediately.

Three plumbers from O'Lawlor Plumbing & Heating visited our house, including the owner. One just started with the company and was still in training. He barely said a thing, although it was difficult for him to get a word in, since the other two plumbers spoke as if they were trying to communicate in the middle of a Megadeath concert. They shouted at the top of their lungs. If the neighbors were unaware of our plumbing issues before this point, they were fully educated on them now.

Christine mentioned that we had called a familiar commercial plumber to snake and scope the sewer line after the backup, and the two men shook their heads, as if rehearsed. "Oh no, no, no," proclaimed Francis O'Lawlor. "You can't go with them ever. They're out here rapin' everybody."

After inspecting the sewer line, both plumbers and their trainee confirmed there were no issues whatsoever with the pipes. "Sure, they're old," Francis said. "Maybe sometime down the line this big cast iron pipe might start leaking and would have to be changed. But not right now and not for twenty thousand dollars. Your sewer line is fine. It's not in dirt. I wouldn't consider replacing them right now."

I laughed at the diagnosis. I found it borderline inhuman yet sitcom-y that two experts in the same field could have polar opposite interpretations of one issue. I suppose that's how you distinguish a scam artist from a genuine expert. One (or three) provided an honest, professional opinion. The other figured he could make a quick twenty Gs off a couple unwitting kids. It's like a dentist diagnosing you with irritable bowel syndrome. You think, *Great, how much is this going to cost me?* After some time passes and a bit of the fog clears from your head, you begin to ask the important questions, like, "Are you even qualified to diagnose that?"

The first plumber made us afraid to even spend time in our own house. I was convinced that if I turned a faucet too much, a pipe might explode and send the house crumbling to the ground, leaving me stuck in a pile of rubble as shit water clogged my windpipes.

Several days later, I visited the spot where the backup happened. I hadn't really looked at the area since the first plumber left. In the corner of the basement were the roots he had pulled out of our pipes—the ones that no one other than he himself had touched. When I picked them up, they weren't as damp as they had been just a few days before. They felt stiff and rough, like something a vegan might make you taste. I bent one of the roots, and it immediately snapped. The inside was light brown, splintered from the snap.

I have done extensive yardwork during my life. I've dug up live trees, dead trees, prickly bushes, and most vegetable plants that can grow in northeastern United States. I've severed live roots and dead roots, but I've never seen one that was ripped from a live tree and dried out completely within a few days. They always seem to stay rubbery and bendable for a while, so much so that they can become makeshift toys for young kids who get bored in the middle of yardwork.

I bent the other root, and it snapped, too. There was no give. The roots just broke like potato chips. This meant that either dead roots were flushed down a toilet in the house, or our original plumber was even less honest than we had realized.

After buying a home and putting the work in to make it livable, I had relied on a three-step plan (that I had unwittingly created) to guide me:

1. Identify the issue(s);
2. Learn how to fix them; and
3. Actually haul ass and fix 'em.

After this ordeal, I found it best to adjust my three-step plan in repairing anything. It's fluid and adaptable, like jazz guitar riffs. Even if you hit the wrong notes, you're still only a step away.

I've since added a fourth step to my guide. I labeled it *2b*. It's not important enough to earn its own number, but it's incredibly significant when it comes to your wallet:

2b. Get a second opinion.

If I want to learn how to change a faucet, I'll watch *two* instructional YouTube videos. If I'd like to grow grass in the dead zone of my backyard, I'll research—and likely utilize—*two* kinds of seeds and fertilizer. If I can't do something at all (which is more common), I'll consult at least *two* experts. Immediately putting all my eggs into one basket is the quickest route to roadside omelets.

I'm no mathematician, but I'd say that about half the people I come in contact with on a daily basis are bullshit artists. Maybe some are generally honest, but a lot of people certainly want unlimited access to my wallet, which at this point just has cobwebs and a key tag that gets me free Jr. Frostys with each purchase at Wendy's.

When there's a problem I can't correct myself, receiving a second opinion cuts down the chances of getting screwed by one of these con artists. Sure, it's a pain in the neck to have to involve another party, because it takes up much more time. But that's still preferable to taking up much more money. The last thing I want to do is flush my hard-earned cash down the toilet and have it snaked out of my sewer line by a Pawl. He'd insist it's crucial that he keep all of the money. "There's just no other option."

MANCHILD

On a Saturday afternoon, four months after moving to Mercer County, New Jersey, Christine and I found ourselves without housework. We *did* have a to-do list the length of a CVS receipt, but on this particular weekend, we made no plans to complete any tasks. We considered it a "mental health" weekend, but really we just were burnt out from pushing ourselves to fix every issue we found with our new seventy-year-old house. That's adulthood: a game of picking up the pieces faster than they can fall. That's the goal, at least. I don't know if anyone ever actually wins.

Christine and I discussed taking a drive along the Delaware River. "We can drive up the Pennsylvania side," I suggested, "stop for dinner somewhere."

"A restaurant in New Hope?" she pleaded. I took it she wasn't in the mood for any surprises, so I agreed.

New Hope, Pennsylvania, is about a forty-five, maybe fifty-minute drive north of Center City Philadelphia. It's a hub of eclectic eateries and specialty shops that typically are favored in cities like Manhattan and San Francisco. Right next to a record store you've got a witch shop; across the street from a candy emporium is a vape outlet, and a couple doors down from there you can get a piercing on any body part you can name. Or after picking up some takeout kadai chicken from a popular Indian restaurant, you can stop to get a psychic reading on the same block. Some shops help to make you inexplicably happy, while others make you feel like you just tossed your wallet into the Delaware.

I drove us through Main Street in New Hope, nearly colliding with at least a half-dozen pedestrians who believed they were too good for concrete sidewalks and deserved the much easier-on-the-hip-replacement pavement of the road. Parking on the side of the street is a hot commodity in the borough, like toilet paper during a pandemic. You'll likely hit seven pedestrians with your car before you find a vacant spot. At least, that was my excuse to Christine as I drove us farther north and out of New Hope, away from the restaurants at which she had wanted to dine. Just north of the city, I crossed a bridge back into New Jersey.

"Let's drive through Lambertville," I suggested. "Maybe it'll be less crowded and we can find a place to park."

Lambertville sits on the New Jersey side of the Delaware River, directly across from New Hope, where the two are joined by a bridge. It's our version of the Pennsylvania borough, just with a little less passion. If the cities were beer, Lambertville would be "New Hope Lite."

I turned onto Bridge Street, immediately taking note of how crowded it was there, too. So I took the New Hope-Lambertville Bridge back over to Pennsylvania. The bridge is a six-span, pin-connected Pratt through truss. It supports two lanes for traffic and a cantilevered walkway on one side for pedestrians.

My parents brought my brothers and me here a handful of times growing up. We'd park in Lambertville and walk the bridge to New Hope and then back. Each time, I'd make jokes about tossing one of my brothers off the bridge, garnering no laughs but my own. "*Patrick*," my father would say, a hard period at the end of the "-ick" to indicate he did not find me funny.

"*What?*" I'd reply with childish incandescence, whistling through the gap of a missing tooth.

On one trip to New Hope, my youngest brother Anthony brought a teddy bear along with him. Anthony was about seven, just beginning first grade. Teddy was the class's inanimate mascot and learned alongside Anthony and his classmates Monday through Friday. During the weekend, one student was assigned to bring the stuffed animal home and take care of him. If the student went on any trips—to the movies, grandma's house, soccer practice—the bear was to tag along. Parents were encouraged to snap photos of Teddy's activities throughout the weekend so that their kids could share them with the class. Had we not ventured to New Hope during Anthony's turn, my mother might've snapped nine photographs of the bear sitting at the kitchen table in front of a different meal she had just prepared. But that weekend my dad suggested we visit New Hope.

As Christine and I drove over the New Hope-Lambertville Bridge, I thought about how my other brother Christopher, eight years old at the time, had tried to convince Anthony to toss Teddy into the river. When coercion didn't work, Chris resorted to physical intervention. He'd nudge Anthony when he was close to the rail and snicker as Anthony pulled the red-shirted stuffed bear closer to his body like a running back with the football on fourth and goal. I wondered what would have happened if Anthony returned to class that Monday morning sans teddy bear.

"He fell into *what*?!" his teacher would demand.

"The Delaware River," Anthony would answer. "If he hasn't gotten caught on a branch yet, he's gotta be halfway to Fishtown by now."

My imagination made me wish I had helped Chris get that teddy bear into the river fourteen years ago. My teenage self would've fed Anthony a number of hackneyed excuses to give his teacher.

"Tell her Teddy just couldn't *bear* the weight of his first-grade responsibilities . . . No, no! Say he saw a gorgeous salmon and just dove in. Oh, wait! Tell her he fell into the river after he lost his *bear*ings!"

I wondered how many times that bear repeated the first grade before the teacher sent him to a fate equal to that of being thrown into the Delaware River. Maybe Chris was just trying to put poor Teddy out of his misery.

Christine and I crossed the bridge, and I pulled into the closest lot just west of the New Hope & Ivyland Railroad. We paid the meter and headed down toward Main Street. Christine and I traded "What are you in the mood for-s" several times before stumbling upon a place with a view of the river.

"Do you have a reservation?" the maître d' asked as we hovered around the host stand.

"No, we don't," Christine told her. "Do we need one?" I looked around the restaurant, which had at least ten open tables that were clean, two that were dirty, and no one waiting around.

"Yes, I'm sorry. We're all booked for the night."

We had the same luck at two other restaurants as we continued along Main Street. We decided to take our chances at a pub near an ice cream parlor my parents had taken me to as a kid. I remembered the place had about a dozen original flavors of homemade ice cream, yet I ordered the vanilla Italian ice for dessert on that first visit. I didn't know it at the time, but that spoke volumes of the child I was and the adult I was doomed to become. My mother was a good sport though, and instead of immediately checking me into the nearest childcare facility, she simply asked, "Are you *sure* that's what you want?"

Standing at the doorway of this roadside pub with uninviting grime coating the knob like sunscreen, I was inclined to ask Christine that same question. But at this point I was getting "hangry" and was in no position to turn my nose up to the first restaurant that hadn't turned us away all night.

After dinner, Christine treated us to dessert at that same ice cream parlor I had visited with my family almost a decade and a half earlier. They scaled back a tad on their selections, but they still offered similar original flavors, like Midnight Jersey, which was just dark chocolate ice cream with caramel and pretzel pieces. I couldn't determine the analogy there, but the pretzel pieces represent either tree branches in the road or the mafia. I haven't made up my mind yet.

While perusing the flavor choices, I happened to notice an inconspicuous sign indicating that the shop still offered Italian ice. It was somewhat obstructed by a poster listing the special coffee-infused milkshakes they now made.

"You have Italian ice?" I asked.

The cashier's face lit up. I must have been the first person to show interest in Italian ice this year while their inventory gradually perished with frostbite. "Oh yes," she said and listed the available flavors, beginning with chocolate. I heard nothing after that first flavor and ordered their largest cup. I obviously couldn't see my expression as the girl behind the counter handed me my order, but I imagine it wasn't much different from how I looked fourteen years prior when I was handed my vanilla Italian ice. If I had shared this moment on social media,

I would've capped it with *#Progress* and an emoji of the praying hands.

Christine and I took the seats near the shop's window overlooking Main Street. Although we couldn't see the river, we watched as people marched along the side of the road, back and forth. Everyone looked disenchanted, almost absent minded, like their bodies were here while they thought about being somewhere else. I blamed it on the altitude. I felt perched a mile high.

"I want to check out the shop next door," Christine said to me as she scooped up the last bit of her raspberry ice cream. "I saw a cute bathing suit I might want to get."

As we approached the storefront, she pointed to a one-piece that hung just outside the window. It looked like it was made entirely of gold sequins. Christine laughed and said she'd like a sparkly bathing suit for our honeymoon. I told her it'd attract the fish, if not human traffickers, and she grimaced.

A middle-aged librarian-looking woman was standing right at the entrance of the store and backed away from us as we entered. "Welcome!" she exclaimed, adjusting her thick-rimmed glasses. "Please let me know if you need anything at all."

Neither Christine nor I moved from the entryway of the shop. The store was tight. It felt about the size of the first-class section on a domestic airline. Clothing and knickknacks were packed onto racks and shelves, with narrow aisles that circled the shop. There was a rack of women's nighttime clothing directly next to me. One top appeared to be made of vertically hung strands of film from a cassette tape. On a stand next to that rack were several solo shoes. One was a glossy silver platform heal six inches high.

Where would those *be appropriate?* I thought.

Christine nudged me. "This is an adult shop," she muttered, low so that the lady who greeted us couldn't hear.

My first thought was, *I'm not allowed to be in here.* Then I remembered that I qualified as an adult. But, for some reason, that didn't make me feel any more welcome.

I looked around the store in one swooping glance and saw that Christine was right. They didn't sell bathing suits here— these were outfits for *other* occasions. The tops and bottoms on the racks in front of me were lacey and tiny. They looked like they were designed for people about the size of an American Girl doll. The attire ranged from neon greens and hot pinks to deep blues and black latex. The mannequins in the windows were arranged provocatively, and one was even cradling a silver pole that ran the length of floor to ceiling. In the back of the store was a wall filled with various intimate toys, mostly pink. I could probably name the use of three of them, but the other eighty-five didn't look like technology frequently found among earthlings.

After quickly surveying the store, my first instinct was to leave, even though I certainly had a right to be there. I recently had gotten married and was in the store with my wife. Other men might've stayed and browsed around to see if there was anything that warranted putting a dent in the Visa bill, but I didn't naturally feel that way. Some of the people who visit New

Hope come to this town for shops like this, but I just want the food and the ice cream—or Italian ice.

I reached for the doorknob of the exit. I imagine I looked like a toddler who was attempting to sneak extra ice pops from the freezer without alerting his parents. For some reason, I didn't want this woman to see me leave. I didn't even want her to know I had entered to begin with. But it was way too late.

When I grabbed the doorknob and began to push the door open, the lady up front said, with a giggle, "Don't worry, boys are allowed in here, too."

The woman called me a "boy," but I wasn't insulted for being referred to as a juvenile. That was my immediate thought about myself too when Christine told me what kind of shop this was. This woman could've easily advised that "men" were allowed in here too, but she chose her words carefully. She answered a question I didn't ask. She knew me even though she never met me. Little did she know, I ordered the *chocolate* Italian ice this time around, so I should've been more prepared than ever to peruse a shop like this. But that wasn't the fuel I needed to stick around, and all I could muster was a waning "Thank you" as I pushed the door wide open and exited, Christine close behind.

SAVED BY THE BELL

Every couple months, Christine wakes me in the middle of the night. All I feel is a nudge to my shoulder or a tap on my chest. Before my eyes can fully open, I hear her shout-whisper, "I thought you were dead!"

As if my wide-open eyes and shaking head aren't enough proof, I feel the need to confirm, "I'm not."

"You weren't moving, and your skin was cold." Then, while rolling over away from me, she'll add, "You scared the crap out of me."

Incidentally, I spend the rest of the early morning hours very much alive and awake in bed, unable to fall back to sleep until moments before my alarm sounds.

I have a fear of being buried alive. Fortunately for me, someone invented the "safety coffin" in the eighteenth century. It was a mechanism that helped to prevent premature burials in the event that someone in a seemingly lifeless slumber was pronounced dead and quickly buried. This device allowed the occupant to pull a cable in the coffin that rang a bell above ground to signal that they were still alive. As it turns out, there was a prominent fear of being buried alive during the cholera outbreaks in the nineteenth century. In the twenty-first century, all we have is COVID apparently, which has heightened my fears at least to some degree, I'll admit.

Therefore, I'd like to be buried in a safety coffin when I "die." Although, in order to avoid being prematurely buried altogether, maybe I should just donate my body to science. I'd like to think that kids studying medicine would be able to identify that I was still alive in the event I was incorrectly declared deceased. I wouldn't mind future doctors, nurses, scientists, and congresspeople (I know they're up to something) running experiments on my lifeless body in order to learn and build experience before they maculate living beings. I wouldn't even care if they used my body as a life-sized marionette doll for choreographed plays in between sessions of dissecting my spleen and locating my pancreas. I do not, however, like the idea of a group of med students fondling my jewels or whatever they do to a cadaver's genitals. If it does turn out I'm still alive, my hope is that we'll know before it gets that far.

After spending many sleepless nights worrying about being buried alive—or otherwise violated by a group of politicians—I thought it was only appropriate that I plan my funeral as well.

The two go hand in hand. These types of life events (or "lack-of-life" events) can really sneak up on you. It's better to be safe than sorry. My mom used to tell me that.

This whole idea actually came about when I Googled myself one day and found my obituary. It wasn't mine, exactly, but rather some other Patrick Lombardi from New Jersey. I read this stranger's entire mortuary tribute and was impressed by how highly he was regarded, but I wondered if any of it was true. Had he really run seven marathons after age sixty and saved a toddler from drowning in a pond? Was he really a volunteer at four nursing homes, even when he was old enough to be a resident at any one of them? Did he really donate his life savings to cancer research? If so, how has he not been canonized yet?

I started drafting my own obituary with the intent that everyone would receive an accurate representation of me. It was less complicated than I had expected, and I finished the entire piece while watching an episode of *3rd Rock from the Sun*. The next logical step was to devise a plan to prevent myself from being buried alive, and *then* I began planning my actual funeral.

It turns out that it's a lot more complex than arranging any other type of party, like a birthday or anniversary celebration. I knew funerals were costly, but I didn't think they'd be so intricate and grueling, specifically when a loved one (or yourself) *hasn't* died yet.

Caskets actually cost a ridiculous amount of money, and I don't find it necessary for my lifeless—or life-*full*—body to be required to rest in such a baroque crate. Some people deserve that; their lives warrant an honorable goodbye. But all I do is write things, some of which make people happy, while most other pieces make people angrier.

After I die, I find it acceptable for my body to be displayed in a cardboard box. The only requirement is that bell-and-pulley system. I'd prefer that those executing my funeral affairs put the rest of that coffin money toward something more useful, like a carnival-sized cotton candy machine, a chocolate fountain modeled after the Trevi Fountain, or a massive piñata in the form of a sprightly alebrije. There may even be space in the funeral home for a fried Oreo and funnel cake station, and in a separate room where mourners flee to cry in private, we can fit a miniature bouncy castle—for the kids. I'd like for my funeral to be a celebration, not unlike a wedding or the birth of a child. I'm sure I can find the chocolate-cigar equivalent for death.

Whether patrons are rejoicing my life or my demise doesn't much concern me. What does concern me, though, is that I won't be able to attend, because it sounds like it's going to be a rager.

Some may believe that planning your own funeral with the same gusto as planning your own wedding illustrates characteristics of a severely corrupt mind. Alternatively, directing your own funeral arrangements may be a sign that a person has to be in control of every single element of his life. But, realistically, it's just more logical.

Take a moment to give it some serious consideration: Death, being inevitable and uncompromising, is often spontaneous. One day you could be on the beach sipping a piña colada, and the next you might find yourself making arrangements for a loved one's burial. No matter how prepared one might be for death, it's something many of us have trouble accepting and something with which countless people never come to terms. The people who do take it lightly are often the ones emailing the Grim Reaper for an ETA. He's not replying, so it's better not to just sit tight and wait. Besides, there are pre-arrangement funeral forms available online to be filled out before you pass. That's evidence right there that I'm not as crazy as you may be thinking right now.

Weddings, on the other hand, don't sneak up on you. You and your significant other give yourselves months or maybe even years of preparation time, which brings to mind another drawback to planning a wedding so far in advance: interests change, enthusiasm fades. You make non-refundable deposits on videographers and caterers you may later decide to release.

Planning your funeral includes less of that stress, because you've made your wishes contractually binding, and it's up to your relatives/friends/the state to bring them to life. No pun intended. If you don't like the way your funeral comes out, who cares? You'll be dead. Nothing about your wedding, though, should be a surprise. You and your significant other designate nearly everything, including the date and time. Until I can set the date of my own death, I'll proceed with planning my funeral under the assumption that one day I'll be surprised to find myself expired.

My wife loathes the term "expired" as an alternative to "died" or "passed away." She says it sounds disrespectful, and I've noticed it makes her cringe whenever someone says it in front of her.

I don't much mind that usage of the word. I would never use it to describe another person's passing, because I agree that it comes off as discourteous, particularly to the bereaved.

That's the problem with the term: Departed souls can't let us know if it's appropriate or not. Or maybe they can, but we're just not listening. Regardless, I think using the term "expired" will be a fitting way to describe *my* death when my time has come.

I imagine my demise will arrive when God spends a Saturday afternoon cleaning out His refrigerator—the one in His garage, not the new stainless-steel one in the kitchen. There I'll be, tucked in the back of the fridge, behind the organic milk and flax seeds. God will push the carton to the side and find me. He'll crane His neck and scratch His chin, and perhaps He'll reach in, pick me up, shake me a bit. Then He'll turn me around to look at my expiration date. "Oh, wow," He'll say. "This went bad months ago. How in My name did I miss that?" Then He'll peel the lid off the trash can, toss me in, and refocus His attention on the rest of the contents in His outside refrigerator.

I need to be prepared for such an occurrence. So when I'm

done planning my own funeral, *then* I'll focus on my life, career, health, and so on. First, though, I really should be prepared with that safety coffin, just in case.

ACKNOWLEDGEMENTS

Someone told me that no one reads the acknowledgements section in books anymore. Apparently, they polled all eight billion people on the planet and discovered that exactly zero of them acknowledge the acknowledgements. I asked my one-year-old what his position was on acknowledgements, and he grunted at me before saying something that sounded like "ass." Because of that remark, I decided to put an acknowledgements section in this book—so that *no one* would read it.

So, to every person—family, friends, colleagues, and strangers—who asked me repeatedly when I was going to publish my next book: thank you. I don't think I'd have the courage or motivation to put this collection out into the world if it weren't for that interest. Even if you were feigning it, I still appreciate the gesture . . .

Thank you to my editor Matthew Schuman, who wouldn't admit that this manuscript was total dog crap and shouldn't see the light of day, but instead turned these ramblings of a madman into a comprehensible collection.

ACKNOWLEDGEMENTS

An enormous shout-out to my beta readers, who provided invaluable feedback and helped to improve every single one of the pieces they laid eyes on: Dr. Michael Stroppa, Dr. Grace Escamilla, Will Lawler, and Daniel Zorovich. Thank you, David Nemec, for those sick author photos that I'll likely be using until I'm in a safety coffin.

I'd like to also thank Liz Young, owner of the Commonplace Reader bookshop in Yardley, Pennsylvania, and the members of her wonderful writers group. You all have helped me improve upon the craft while also having fun doing it. And thank you to those who took the time to read and provide a blurb for *Clear As Clay*—your kind, thoughtful words mean a lot.

Additionally, my parents and brothers get teased a tiny bit within these pages, so I wanted to add that I appreciate you all providing me great content throughout the last three decades, and I thank you for being great sports and perpetually supportive.

I'd also like to acknowledge Baby Lombardi, who did most of the proofreading and rewriting for this collection. He formatted the interior pages, selected the fonts, and designed the cover. He was my harshest, albeit cutest, critic; there was some shouting and some language I didn't understand, but he always got his point across. Thank you for your support.

Finally, for my first reader, Christine, who read every line before any other person and spent so much time providing input: I can't express how much your continuous encouragement means to me. These essays would've remained buried in a subfolder of a subfolder of a subfolder on my laptop without your acclaim. (So I hope you weren't lying.)

CLEAR AS CLAY

provoking life's moldable moments

This reader's book club edition of *Clear As Clay: Provoking Life's Moldable Moments* includes discussion questions, a conversation with Patrick Lombardi, and the author's recommendations for nonfiction books. The listed questions are intended to help your book club find new perspectives and topics in order to enhance your discussions.

We hope these fresh, engaging insights will help to boost your discussions and elevate your enjoyment of this book!

READER'S BOOK CLUB

DISCUSSION QUESTIONS TO ENHANCE YOUR BOOK CLUB

1. How does the humor in *Clear As Clay* help us to navigate some of the book's more serious situations, such as miscarriages, self-doubt, and daily struggles? Do you think, in covering these particular subject matters, Patrick Lombardi was successful in being sensitive and sympathetic to those involved?

2. How does the book challenge traditional notions of adulthood and family dynamics through its humor and storytelling? Does the author accept it or seek to push the envelope with his views and decisions?

3. In "Sampling Safari" and "The Gift," the author highlights impatience and frustration with others. How do you think societal and technological changes have altered our patience?

4. Road rage is a common phenomenon, yet often not discussed openly in detail. How does the book handle this topic, and what insights did it provide?

5. In "The Hungry Turtle," Patrick illustrates how his upbringing impacted his creativity. Were you a creative child? If so, how has your creativity evolved as you became an adult? If not, in which ways did your parents and upbringing influence the figurative paths you've traveled in life?

6. Reflect on the ways in which the book challenges stereotypes about adulthood and family life. How do these challenges contribute to the book's comedy and depth?

7. Humor is often used as a coping mechanism for dealing with difficult situations. How does humor serve as a tool for resilience and healing in your own life? Does anything Patrick described resonate with you and your own sense of humor?

8. Reflect on how the themes of this book relate to your own experiences of adulthood and growing older. How does the author's humor offer fresh perspectives on these universal themes?

9. The author never mentions the title *Clear As Clay* in any essay in the book. What is your own interpretation of the title? After finishing this book, do you find that the author justified or reinforced this message?

10. Next month, read one of Patrick's recommended titles with your book club. Compare the forms of nonfiction and describe which one appeals to you more. Can you relate to one author more than the other? Do their actions, experiences, or perspectives speak to you more than the other?

A CONVERSATION
WITH PATRICK LOMBARDI

Your book explores the journey of becoming an adult—or hoping that you're actually becoming an adult. What aspect of adulthood do you find the most challenging, and how does humor help in coping with it?

Knowing that so much is out of your control is terrifying [laughs]. On the road, in the workplace, even just running errands—so much is out of our hands. As kids and as teenagers, we (or at least I) felt in control and invincible. The older I've gotten, the less I feel that way.

Humor can make us face something that's ugly or uncomfortable. There are many forms of humor—and many senses of humor—so I'm generalizing. But joking or utilizing a form of humor to discuss a serious or unfortunate topic enables me to think about it, instead of trying to block it out and never deal with the issue. When I'm writing about a more serious event, like in "The Problem Is . . .," I'm forced to relive my experiences, my interpretation of other people's experiences, and the events that unfolded; I look at everything with fresher eyes, which helps me extrapolate and appreciate any of the good that was revealed. It's therapeutic, because in instances when I'm not reflecting, I noticed I simply categorize the event as "unfortunate," file it to the back of my mind, and only perpetuate a sourer outlook in the future.

How did you navigate the fine line between humor and sensitivity when discussing subjects like miscarriages and family dynamics?

I had to consider the sense of humor of the people featured in the essays. I have a pretty dark sense of humor at times, and it's hard for me to get offended, so I can get twisted when making fun of my road rage or my insecurities. When other people appear in my writing—particularly my writing that's for public consumption—I have to dial back that intensity, and I think about how those individuals would feel reading these stories.

For example, when writing "The Problem Is . . ." I tried to put myself in my wife's shoes. The essay is written from my point of view, of course, but I wanted to be sensitive to the situation. During that time, she used some humor to help herself grieve, and I included some of that in the piece. More than a year passed between writing that essay and revisiting, revising, and editing it—and our son was born—so I was able to look at it with fresher eyes and a new perspective and really give that subject matter the voice it deserves.

On the other hand—to answer the "family dynamics" part—my mom, who appears in a few more essays in this book, has thick skin and a dark sense of humor like me. So I didn't really hold back [laughs].

Throughout the book, you occasionally mention being a father, and there's only one essay about the subject. Was it a conscious decision to leave any stories about parenthood out of this collection?

For the most part, yes. The truth is, I haven't written any other essays about parenthood, so it's not like I have a trove of unused essays. My son's still a baby, and while so much has happened over the past near-two years, I know there is so much more ahead. Maybe that's a book by itself, but I'd like to keep all those stories and experiences private, at least until he's old enough to understand.

Work is often a source of stress in many people's lives. How do you balance the comedic aspects of work with its more serious overtones?

Over the years, I've worked with a lot of great people. Work can get overwhelming and stressful, but I've had plenty of support along the way, which I'm grateful for. It's allowed me some brief opportunities to breathe and take a look around me and capture those humorous moments. The only way I can really make light of certain work situations in my writing is by omitting those serious challenges. When events are simplified, I can highlight the lighter moments a bit better. Writing is a nice outlet for that, because then when I'm at work, I can focus on my responsibilities and leave those stories at home.

During your writing process, did you draw inspiration from any particular comedians or authors known for blending humor with personal experiences?

My biggest influence in writing this style is David Sedaris. I've been reading his essays for years and have always enjoyed his voice and found it hilarious. His writing is so crisp and witty; he can make any situation sound interesting. Dave Barry is another author who's influenced this book. His latest book, *Lessons From Lucy*, offers a bit of life advice (and of course "lessons") mixed in with the humor, and as a reader, I took so much out of it. I wanted to give readers some of that, too.

In terms of comedians, I discovered Nate Bargatze after all of these essays were already written (maybe with the exception of "The Problem Is . . ."); however, his voice really snuck in during the editing process. Aside from being absolutely hilarious, he gets to the point without a lot of preamble, yet you always know what he's talking about or can relate in some way. I was able to trim a lot of the fat in my essays by thinking about his technique and delivery.

What was the most surprising or unexpected aspect of writing a humor book centered on such personal and sometimes difficult topics?
I was a lot more open than I thought I could be. When I'd go back and read some of these essays, I'd often cringe at something I did, said, or even thought, and as much as I wanted to remove certain parts, I knew that was a sign that I couldn't [laughs]. There were a lot of internal battles, but a lot of the embarrassment had to remain. Although I still am conflicted, I think the book is funnier because of it. For better or worse, you get many sides of Patrick Lombardi when you read *Clear As Clay*.

What's your word of advice to other writers who are struggling with opening up in a similar fashion?
Don't plan to show anyone what you've written—not a single soul. I like to imagine that I'm writing to a single person, rather

than an entire audience, which helps me keep the tone conversational and also prevents me from really holding back. But every time I write, I keep the mindset that no one will see it. When I revisit a piece for revision, maybe then I can touch it up if I plan to publish, but otherwise it's always mine. That's the best way I've found to stay genuine.

Also, don't tell people what you're writing while you're still writing it. Just don't. Maybe I'm superstitious and believe that if I tell someone the subject or synopsis of the story I'm writing, then I won't finish it or it won't come out well—or maybe they'll steal the idea and write it first and get a book deal with Simon & Schuster and become an international bestseller! Or maybe I'm just paranoid . . . Either way, keep your writing to yourself until it's all done so that there's no possibility of anyone's thoughts, ideas, or facial expressions altering your progress.

What do you hope readers take away from your book, particularly regarding the more serious topics you address with humor?

Don't always take yourself so seriously. Be passionate—be thoughtful and sincere and deliberate—but take time to laugh at yourself. You're not always right or deep or intellectual, so don't beat yourself up when you make mistakes or fall short of your goal. Have fun with your loved ones; make a positive impact with your colleagues; and, as a wise man once sang in a gorgeous tenor, "be good to yourself" (credits to Journey on that last one).

THE AUTHOR RECOMMENDS: NONFICTION

I grew up on fiction. As a kid, it was Shel Silverstein and *Magic Tree House*, before morphing into Goosebumps and *A Series of Unfortunate Events*. That eventually led to Stephen King, H.P. Lovecraft, Harlan Coben, and Kurt Vonnegut. In college, I discovered David Sedaris, and humor was all I wanted to read for years. Nonfiction grew on me then, too. The genre's not just stuffy memoirs and drab textbooks—there's a lot of depth and variety.

Since *Clear As Clay* is nonfiction, I figured the right thing to do was suggest other nonfiction titles. Even if you hated this book, I'm sure you'll enjoy a lot of what is on this list, depending on your taste. These are mostly humor, but I tried to switch it up a bit. Also, this is by no means an exhaustive list. There are a number of other incredible nonfiction titles out there that I may have temporarily forgotten about (or not even read . . .), but these are a few of my recent favorites. Enjoy!

- **David Sedaris: *Me Talk Pretty One Day***
  If you picked up this book, chances are you've already heard of *Me Talk Pretty One Day* or at least David Sedaris. From beginning to end, this is one of the funniest books out there. In the first part, Sedaris shares his upbringing in Raleigh, North Carolina, while the

second is mostly about his (then-current) life in Normandy, France, with his partner. The title is a recurring theme, and this was a huge inspiration for the essays in *Clear As Clay*.

- **Dave Barry:** *Lessons From Lucy: The Simple Joys of an Old, Happy Dog*
  I've loved Dave Barry's stuff over the years, but this has become my favorite. Barry shares the lessons he's learned about life and aging from his dog Lucy. The book is mostly joyful in tone, but Barry shares some challenges that resonate. He can be serious and humorous, and he blends those styles really well in this book.

- **Mike Birbiglia:** *Sleepwalk with Me: And Other Painfully True Stories*
  Standup comic Mike Birbiglia put this collection together, willingly sharing embarrassing stories from his life. The title is based on a sleeping disorder he discovered during adulthood—but I'll let him tell you about it. Hilarious from beginning to end, *Sleepwalk with Me* reads like a crisp standup routine.

- **Mindy Kaling:** *Is Everyone Hanging Out Without Me? (And Other Concerns)*
  I'll admit, I mainly picked up this book because I'm a huge *Office* fan and knew how significantly Mindy Kaling had contributed to the show behind the scenes.

So I had a good feeling I would enjoy this book. Although it didn't have me rolling on the floor, Kaling is still as hilarious on the page as she is on screen. Her stories are interesting and engaging, making this an excellent collection for all humor fans.

- **Dave Grohl:** *The Storyteller: Tales of Life and Music*
As a big Foo Fighters fan, I had to read this regardless of whether Dave Grohl really is a "storyteller." Fortunately, he is, breathing life into the tales of his upbringing, early musical days, and rock and roll. I recommend for any music fan.

- **Jason Gay:** *Little Victories: A Sportswriter's Notes on Winning at Life*
Jason Gay's debut book helped to mold the essays in *Clear As Clay*. His writing is funny and clean, describing his life and career in engaging details. It's not a self-help book, but more memoir/humor. Right up your alley if you enjoyed my book.

- **Bonnie McFarlane:** *You're Better Than Me*
Another witty comic's memoir. Bonnie McFarlane shares bits about her life, career, and the struggles and successes of pursuing your passion. She's blunt and doesn't pull any punches, only making her accounts even funnier.

- **Robin Roberts:** *Everybody's Got Something*
  This was the first of Robin Roberts's books that I read, which may be why it has stuck with me the most. Her voice is positive and inspiring, despite the challenges she has faced in recent years. She is honest and portrays every account with a motivational twist.

- **Tom Segura:** *I'd Like to Play Alone, Please*
  Tom Segura's newest book reads like his standup: crisp and hilarious. Like other comics on this list, he is straightforward, giving readers his unedited views of certain subject matters while mostly sharing stories from his life and career in standup comedy.

- **Michelle Kuo:** *Reading with Patrick: A Teacher, a Student, and a Life-Changing Friendship*
  I'll admit that I read this one because my name is Patrick and I like to read. However, I did wind up enjoying Michelle Kuo's story. She taught two years of middle school in Alabama before earning a degree in law. She discussed the struggles her students faced at school and at home and how she was able to connect with them, including Patrick.

- **James McBride:** *The Color of Water: A Black Man's Tribute to His White Mother*
  I find it amazing how James McBride is able to incorporate so much about his and his mother's lives in this

short book. He uses few words to convey so much information and emotion. It's a compelling, gripping memoir, covering themes of identity, introspection, racism, and family. Even though it was published more than 25 years ago, it's still poignant today.

- **Dr. Lise Deguire:** *Flashback Girl: Lessons on Resilience from a Burn Survivor*
  This is the true life story of Dr. Lise Deguire, Psy.D., who suffered third-degree burns on 65 percent of her body when she was four years old. The following decades of her life offered more tragedy and trauma. Despite this, Deguire is able to share countless life lessons and positive outlooks in the tale of her life. *Flashback Girl* is a moving piece of nonfiction from start to end.

Praise for Patrick Lombardi's debut book

Junk Sale: Stories & Essays

"A refreshing take on an old short story theme . . . [E]very tale has a sense of ironic humour that makes you want to read the next story to see what this guy is going to come up with next."
— **Gordon A. Long,** *Airborn Press*

"*Junk Sale* attests to the author's keen observation of people without being a busybody. Brutal honesty is what he is going for in writing this book."
— **Vincent Dublado,** *Readers' Favorite*

"Full of razor-sharp wit and driven by a hyper-contemporary voice, *Junk Sale* by Patrick Lombardi is a wickedly smart and hilarious collection of short stories and essays."
— *Self-Publishing Review*

"While I have not read this book, I certainly have it in my house. I think. And you can quote me on that."
— **James Murray,** *Impractical Jokers*

Find Patrick online!

Visit
patricklombardi.com

Facebook: @PatrickLombardiWriter
Instagram: @patlombardi4
TikTok: @patrick.lombardi
Twitter/X: @patlombardi4